John Lennon

"Imagine"

Read about other
American REBELS

Andy Warhol
"Everyone Will be Famous for 15 Minutes"

ISBN-13: 978-0-7660-3385-6

Elvis Presley
"I Want to Entertain People"

ISBN-13: 978-0-7660-3382-5

James Dean
"Dream As If You'll Live Forever"

ISBN-10: 0-7660-2537-3

Jimi Hendrix
"Kiss The Sky"

ISBN-10: 0-7660-2449-0

Johnny Cash
"The Man in Black"

ISBN-13: 978-0-7660-3386-3

Kurt Cobain
"Oh Well, Whatever, Nevermind"

ISBN-10: 0-7660-2426-1

Madonna
"Express Yourself"

ISBN-10: 0-7660-2442-3

Malcolm X
"I Believe in the Brotherhood of Man, All Men"

ISBN-13: 978-0-7660-3384-9

Muhammad Ali
"I am the greatest"

ISBN-13: 978-0-7660-3381-8

John Lennon

"Imagine"

Jeff Burlingame

Enslow Publishers, Inc.
40 Industrial Road
Box 398
Berkeley Heights, NJ 07922
USA

http://www.enslow.com

Library of Congress Cataloging-in-Publication Data

Burlingame, Jeff.
　John Lennon : "Imagine" / Jeff Burlingame.
　　p. cm. — (American rebels)
　Summary: "A biography of British-born rock-and-roll legend John Lennon, who lived and died in New York City. This book discusses his early life, rise and fall of the Beatles, personal hardships, and legacy"—Provided by publisher.
　Includes bibliographical references and index.
　ISBN 978-0-7660-3675-8
　1. Lennon, John, 1940–1980—Juvenile literature. 2. Rock musicians—England—Biography—Juvenile literature. 3. Beatles—Juvenile literature. I. Title.
　ML3930.L34B87 2011
　782.42166092—dc22
　[B]   2009040045

Printed in the United States of America

052010 Lake Book Manufacturing, Inc., Melrose Park, IL

10 9 8 7 6 5 4 3 2 1

To Our Readers: This book has not been authorized by John Lennon's estate or its successors.

We have done our best to make sure all Internet addresses in this book were active and appropriate when we went to press. However, the author and the publisher have no control over and assume no liability for the material available on those Internet sites or on other Web sites they may link to. Any comments or suggestions can be sent by e-mail to comments@enslow.com or to the address on the back cover.

♻ Enslow Publishers, Inc., is committed to printing our books on recycled paper. The paper in every book contains 10% to 30% post-consumer waste (PCW). The cover board on the outside of each book contains 100% PCW. Our goal is to do our part to help young people and the environment too!

Photo Credits: © ArenaPal/Topham/The Image Works, p. 75; Associated Press, pp. 9, 46, 82, 117, 131, 134, 137; CBS/Landov, p. 11; Andy Crowder, p. 23; EMPICS/Landov, p. 110; Everett Collection, pp. 98, 128; Bob Gruen, p. 125; © Tom Hanley/Alamy, p. 27; Michael Ochs Archives/Getty Images, p. 38; Mirrorpix/Courtesy Everett Collection, pp. 101, 113; PA Photos/Landov, p. 139; Redferns/Getty Images, pp. 17, 69; Rue des Archives/The Granger Collection, New York, p. 63; Joy Renee Selnick, p. 1; Shutterstock, p. 135; Andy Vorzimer, p. 56.

Cover Photo: Bob Gruen.

Contents

Chapter 1

Coming to America

The euphoria had faded, and the nerves had taken over. It had been several hours since the girls had screamed and sobbed for them. It had been 3,500 miles since their plane had left the London airport, each second of its ascent shrinking the thousands of song-singing Britons below, until their "We Love You, Beatles"[1] signs no longer could be seen from the windows of Pan Am Flight 101.

The pre-takeoff passion on February 7, 1964, had been expected. The Beatles were England's biggest rock and roll band, heading off to America for the first time to try to succeed in a country where so many other British bands had failed. America was a difficult market to penetrate. Rock and roll music had been invented there. It was home to groundbreaking musicians such as Chuck Berry, Bob Dylan, and Elvis Presley. Those were the people the four Beatles had grown up listening to and had drawn their inspiration from. Those were the people they had idolized.

As New York City came into view, George Harrison was sick with the flu, but he still worried about the looks of his poufy hairdo.[2] Ringo Starr said he and his bandmates "did all feel a bit sick. . . . Going to the States was a big step. People said just because we were popular in Britain, why should we be there?"[3] Paul McCartney wondered the same thing: "What are we going to give [Americans] that they don't already have?"[4]

As the Beatles' outspoken leader, John Lennon also had questions. He wondered exactly what the trip to America would hold for him and his three bandmates. Before the plane took off, he had said, "I just hope we go all right."[5] During the flight he said, "We can always turn around and go home again if no one likes us."[6] Years later, he admitted the full extent of his pre-voyage fears: "We didn't think we stood a chance."[7]

Many of the Beatles' fears may have been calmed had they known exactly how much publicity they had been receiving in the United States. They knew that just a few days earlier their single, "I Want to Hold Your Hand," had become the number one record in America. But they did not know their record label had spent fifty-thousand dollars on a campaign to spread word of their impending arrival. They did not know that five million "The Beatles Are Coming" stickers had been plastered across the United States, nor did they know that fifty

The Beatles giving a press conference in
JFK International Airport in 1964.

thousand people had applied for the 728 seats available to see them perform on *The Ed Sullivan Show*.

As the plane began its descent into New York City, the pilot took notice of what was going on below. He said, "Tell the boys there's a big crowd waiting for them."[8] That was an understatement. Roughly ten thousand people, mostly teenagers, were waiting at the John F. Kennedy International Airport terminal. Girls screamed, and also sobbed, as they held signs welcoming the band to America. The crowd chanted the songs of their soon-to-be heroes, and sang a popular novelty song called, "We Love You Beatles."

Screams filled the air as the Beatles exited the plane and were ushered to a press conference inside the airport. The room was full of reporters, who began firing off questions as soon as the band members walked in. It was near chaos, but with his first words, Lennon took control: "Everybody just *sharrup* [shut up]."[9] The media applauded, then did just as Lennon asked. The questions came at rapid fire and the Beatles handled them all with the sarcastic wit that had helped make the band so endearing in Europe:

"Will you please sing something?"
All four Beatles: "No!"
"Is that because you can't sing?"
Lennon: "No, we need money first."
"Why does [your music] excite [people] so much?"
McCartney: "We don't know, really."
Lennon: "If we knew, we'd form another group and be managers."[10]

The Beatles performed on *The Ed Sullivan Show* in 1964. From left to right: Paul McCartney, George Harrison, John Lennon, and Ringo Starr.

The Beatles' most-immediate question had been answered. America had turned out to see the Beatles, and eventually fell for them as hard as their own country had. But Lennon was not satisfied with all that. He also had deeper issues on his mind. Exactly *why* were all these people here to see them? Who were these businessmen clamoring for permission to market Beatles dolls, Beatles wigs, and Beatles lunch boxes? Were people really listening to his music, or were they just caught up in the hype of it all?

For Lennon, the answer to the last question already was clear. He said, "What we generated was fantastic when we played straight rock, and there was nobody to touch us in Britain. But as soon as we made it, the edges were all knocked off. . . . [W]e made it very, very big. We sold out. . . . The Beatles' music died then. . . . We killed ourselves then to make it—and that was the end of it."[11]

But before there could be an end there had to be a beginning. For the Beatles in America, that came on a winter day in 1964, when their silver-winged jet delivered Beatlemania to U.S. soil for the first time. Lennon's beginning came nearly a quarter-century earlier in a war-torn English city as gritty and staunch as he. Both stories are as compelling as any ever told. There are twists. There are shouts. There is love.

Chapter 2

Genius and Pain

The deadliest battle in history was well under way by fall 1940. Much of Asia and Europe had been decimated by Germany, Japan, and their allies, and tens of thousands of people had been killed. What had begun a year earlier with Germany's invasion of Poland had expanded into the Second World War. Fighting was widespread, and heavy in the English port city of Liverpool, where John Winston Lennon was born October 9.

At the time of his birth, John's country was in the midst of the infamous Battle of Britain, the name given to Germany's all-air campaign against England. The German air force, the Luftwaffe, eventually was held at bay by Britain's Royal Air Force, but not before substantial damage was inflicted on England. As a major seaport located on Britain's northwestern coast, Liverpool—and its many manufacturing and shipping areas—was one of the most-attacked and most-affected areas of the entire war.

Many believe John's birth at the Oxford Street Maternity Hospital came during the middle of a ferocious air raid; that his mother, Julia, was in labor in the hospital as her relatives rushed through Liverpool's darkened streets—covering their ears from the piercing air-raid sirens—to be there for her. John's aunt, Mimi Smith, helped that story gain traction when she said years later, "I was dodging in doorways between running as fast as my legs would carry me. . . . There was shrapnel falling and gunfire . . . and when there was a little lull I ran into the hospital ward and there was this beautiful little baby."[1]

The facts, however, seem to contradict Smith's story. The *Liverpool Echo* newspaper, for example, reported that the day *after* John was born: "Two hospitals, a convent, a home for elderly people and a cinema all narrowly escaped serious damage when enemy raiders were over [the town]. . . ."[2] But the paper reported nothing of attacks on the city on John's actual birthday.

Whether or not he was born during an actual air raid, the effects of war were certainly all around John's birth city. Photos from the time show many holes in Liverpool's skyline, where multistory buildings used to stand. Burned-out buildings and blackened rooftops dot the landscape. The Luftwaffe air raids left Liverpool forever scarred. One author described the city as having: "Rows of dirty, terraced houses squashed shoulder to shoulder, flanking torn and badly surfaced roads; alleys rank with bad sewers, dog turds and rats; whilst above it all rear the grim monoliths of chimneys gazing down in blank, brooding silence."[3]

John's middle name was given to him in honor of Britain's recently appointed prime minister, Winston Churchill, the half-American war expert who held England's fate in his hands. It was a name the young child would grow to hate for its connection to a man so linked with war.

John's father, Alfred "Alf" Lennon, was not at the hospital for his son's birth. It was not the bombs that kept him away from the hospital, but rather his job. He was away at sea, where he worked in the merchant marines as a ship's steward. His absence at his first son's birth was not surprising. Alf Lennon had been away much of his two-year marriage to Julia; a fact the new mother's family took much pleasure in noting. None of the family cared for him much. Alf Lennon's father had died when he was young, and his mother—though she worked from dawn to dusk to try to do so—could not support him and his five siblings. Alf Lennon was sent to live in a Liverpool orphanage, leaving there at age fifteen for a job as a waiter on a ship. Not exactly the type of person most parents wish for their daughter to marry.

Julia, on the other hand, was raised by a family whose means far surpassed those of her future

> **John's middle name was given to him in honor of Britain's recently appointed prime minister, Winston Churchill . . .**

husband's. Like Alf Lennon, Julia's father, George Stanley, also made his living off the sea. But George Stanley's work at the Liverpool and Glasgow Tug Salvage Company placed him in the company of people higher up the social ladder. No one in the family could understand why Julia would marry someone like Alf Lennon. Her sister said, "Why she picked [Alf] I'll never know. . . . I couldn't believe she ended up with a seaman. He was a good-for-nothing . . . the type to have one [woman] in every port. Fly-by-night is what I called him."[4]

Though her family did not see any redeeming qualities in Alf Lennon, Julia had almost immediately. It was his intellect and wit that first struck her, along with his boyish good looks. Julia was able to see past Alf's short stature, caused by a battle with rickets as a child. The leg braces he was forced to wear as a remedy left Alf Lennon at just five feet, four inches tall, but his happy-go-lucky attitude more than made up for his shortness in Julia's mind. One relative said, "Anywhere Freddie [Alf] turned up always meant fun was about to start. He couldn't resist having a good time."[5] He also was a talented musician. At fourteen, Alf Lennon had run away from his orphanage to join a children's musical show—and was severely punished upon his return. He also sang and played the banjo, the latter a skill which Julia herself had learned from her grandfather.

The pair met in 1930, when Alf was fifteen and Julia fourteen. The couple's courtship lasted eight years, lengthened no doubt by Alf's stints at sea, which kept

John Lennon and his mother in the late 1940s.

him from seeing Julia for months at a time. But the relationship still progressed. During Alf's time ashore in December 1938, he and Julia secretly wed at the Mount Pleasant Registry Office. No one from the bride's family was there, but Julia made sure it would not be long before they got the news. As soon as she came home, she announced to her father, "There! I've married him,"[6] and waved her marriage license in the air. As might be expected, George Stanley was furious with his daughter. In time, however, he decided he may as well do his part to make the best of a bad situation, and he moved the rest of his immediate family out of their three-bedroom house at 9 Newcastle Road so the newlyweds could make it their own home.

Stanley's hope that the gift would get the couple off on the right foot was offset by Julia's behavior. Bored and lonely with a husband at sea, Julia grew restless, and she began venturing out at night to Liverpool's numerous pubs and dance halls. There, she soon met a Welsh soldier named Taffy Williams, and she became pregnant with his child in 1944. John was four years old at the time; his mother was thirty.

For a while, Alf Lennon remained oblivious to his wife's extramarital relationship. Still away at sea, Lennon continued sending romantic letters and paychecks home to his wife and his son. But soon he began having his own major issues to deal with. Twice he was sent to prison for various misdeeds and, at one point, the British navy mailed a letter to Julia saying they had no idea where her husband was. It was not until late 1944 that he turned up at home, only to discover his wife was pregnant by another man. Lennon tried to save his marriage and keep the family intact, even offering to raise his wife's new child as his own and forgive her for her indiscretions. None of it worked. Julia Lennon no longer had feelings for the man she had been together with for more than a decade. One family member later hypothesized as to the cause: "Alf reappeared intermittently with various excuses—and took off again. . . . [Mother] had had enough of her on-off marriage. She was young and fun and full of life and she obviously wanted more from a husband than Alf had to offer. . . . [Mother] was never sure of anything about Alf. His inability to commit himself was doubtless influenced by his emotionally deprived upbringing."[7]

But [John] was aware that his father only came by for brief visits, and that there was turmoil in the household when he did so.

When Julia gave birth to a daughter, Victoria Elizabeth, in June 1945, her relationship with Alf was all but over. Hurt and humbled, Alf returned to his job at sea. George Stanley, embarrassed by his daughter, Julia, giving birth to an illegitimate child, insisted that Victoria be given up for adoption. Julia reluctantly agreed, and she returned to her partying ways.

Not yet five years old when all this happened, John did not know much of what was going on. By all accounts, he was unaware at the time that his mother had even had another child. But he was aware that his father only came by for brief visits, and that there was turmoil in the household when he did so.

The following year, John's mother became involved with another man, a somewhat older hotel worker named Bobby Dykins, and the couple soon moved in together. Julia's family and friends did not like Dykins, either. They described the new suitor as having a violent temper with "a very short fuse. Julia knew when to get out of his way, but occasionally he would lash out and slap her."[8] John later said one of his most-vivid childhood memories included the time when "my mother came to see us in a black coat with her face bleeding."[9]

In addition, and partly because of the abuse he had to witness at home, John was forced to make a tough decision the summer prior to his sixth birthday. His father had quit his job as a ship's steward—where he was traversing the Atlantic between southern England and New York—and had returned to Liverpool to take his son for the day. He took John to the northwestern town of Blackpool, England, and lavished junk food and gifts on the boy. But the day-long adventure turned into weeks, and Alf had not returned John home. Angered and upset, Julia and Bobby Dykins eventually found out where the pair was, and they traveled to Blackpool to take John back. When they got there, Alf asked his son a question no young boy should have to answer: Did he want to go with his mother or stay with his father? John was understandably torn. In the words of biographer Phillip Norman: "John went to Alf and took his hand;

then, as Julia turned away again, he panicked and ran after her, shouting to her to wait and to his father to come, too. But, paralyzed once more by fatalistic self-pity, Alf remained rooted in his chair. Julia and John left the house. . . ."[10]

Julia took her son back to Liverpool, but not to live with her and Dykins. Instead, she delivered him to his aunt Mimi's, where he would remain for the rest of his childhood. John later said, "I soon forgot my father. It was like he was dead."[11] He was not, of course, but his relationship with his son basically was. John would not see his father again until after he had become famous. As for his mom, John said, "I did see my mother now and again and my feeling never died off for her. I often thought about her, though I never realized that all the time she was living no more than five or ten miles away. Mimi never told me. She said she was a long, long way away."[12]

John's aunt had her reasons for keeping her youngest sister at a distance. She felt that she—along with her husband, George Smith—offered her nephew the best chance at a proper, trouble-free upbringing. She said, "I just wanted to protect him from all that. Perhaps I was overanxious. I don't know. I just wanted him to be happy."[13]

Aunt Mimi, as John called her, was the opposite of her younger sister, Julia. She was childless and stubborn,

Alf asked his son a question no young boy should have to answer: Did he want to go with his mother or stay with his father?

but responsible, and determined to offer her nephew a stable, if strict, upbringing. John initially thrived under these conditions. The trio lived at Mendips, the name given to the family home on Menlove Avenue in the Liverpool suburb of Woolton. The Smiths' home took its nickname from The Mendip Hills, a geographically diverse area in southwest England. The semidetached, four-bedroom stucco home was comfortable, and John was given the bedroom above the front porch. His half sister said his room "was a real boy's room, as untidy as the rest of the house was immaculately neat. Books were everywhere. . . . Over his bed was a collection of cut-out skeletons and various monsters he had made."[14]

John and jovial Uncle George quickly formed the father-son-type relationship. George provided John with an escape from the strictness of his aunt. But even at a young age, John had a serious side, too. He took a liking to Aunt Mimi's numerous classic novels, spending hours reading them, and soon he began doing some writing and drawing of his own. That love of art continued at nearby Dovedale Primary School, where John won many awards for his drawings.

At seven, John was diagnosed as nearsighted and given glasses, which he did not like wearing. After school, he would wander through the neighborhood, one of his favorite play places being a mansion-turned-orphanage named Strawberry Field. John often would stare through the strawberry-colored iron gates at the home's entrance, and he attended the fund-raising carnival there every summer.

Outside the gate of Strawberry Field as it looks today.

Many historians have reported that John's childhood was much like those of the orphans living at Strawberry Field—a life was filled with depravity, torment, and struggle. But John said that was not true, and that Mimi and George Smith likely had saved him from such a life. He said, "This image of me being the orphan is garbage, because I was well protected by my auntie and my uncle, and they looked after me very well, thanks."[15]

At times, John did struggle to fit in, mostly because he was having difficulty finding an outlet for his creative personality. This often caused him to rebel against authority, as his childhood friend Pete Shotton would later relate. The blond, curly-haired Shotton grew up around the corner from John and was the leader of a small gang of neighborhood boys that included Nigel Whalley and Ivan Vaughan. That is until John moved into the area. Whalley said, "John was always the leader. He was always the one to dare you. He never cared what he said or did. He'd think nothing of putting a brick through the glass in a street lamp. He'd dare us to . . . [try] to hit golf balls across Menlove Avenue. Once, the police came and chased us off. We'd pick up these great clods of earth to chuck at the trains . . . [and put] stuff on the tram rails to try to derail the trams."[16]

Shotton later remembered his earliest recollections of John. He wrote: "This sandy-haired kid with the ridiculous round glasses proved, almost from the start, to be what our parents would have labeled a 'disruptive influence.' Not only was he larger, stronger, and more aggressive than the rest of us, he also seemed a lot wiser to the way of the big bad world."[17] Shotton's assessment was correct. John had experienced more drama in his life than had most children his age, especially those living in the middle-class suburbs he was now a part of. His father was not in his life. His mother was in and out of it. By this time, she was sporadically stopping by Mendips for short visits, only to leave her son with his aunt and uncle when she returned home to the new family she had created with Bobby Dykins. That family included two daughters: Julia, born in 1947, and Jacqueline, born in 1949.

At first, John did not appear bitter about being the odd child out in his mother's life. He attended Sunday school with his friends at St. Peter's Parish Church and enjoyed doing so. But, as would many children in his situation, he soon began acting out. John's outspokenness and ever-expanding dirty vocabulary occasionally got him into trouble at church.

> **"I was aggressive because I wanted to be popular. I wanted to be a leader."**

That trouble followed John to Quarry Bank High School, which he began attending in 1952. John later recalled his first day at the school:

> I looked at all the hundreds of new kids and thought, Christ, I'll have to fight my way through this lot. . . . There was some real heavies there. The first fight I got in I lost. I lost me nerve when I got really hurt. Not that there was much real fighting. I did a lot of swearing and shouting, then

25

got a quick punch. . . . I was aggressive because I wanted to be popular. I wanted to be the leader. I wanted everybody to do what I told them to do, to laugh at my jokes and let me be the boss.[18]

Even the corporal punishment administered by the teachers at the all-boys school did not stop John from misbehaving. He began his first year at Quarry Bank [which is equivalent to the seventh grade in the United States] as a top student, placed in what was called the "A" class, along with his best friend, Pete Shotton. As the years wore on, Shotton recalled the pair had clowned around and neglected their studies so frequently that they were moved down to the lowest-possible class, the "C" level "among the hardcore troublemakers, deadbeats, and halfwits."[19]

> **It was not one specific incident that turned John from a top scholar to a "deadbeat" and "halfwit," rather it was a combination of events.**

It was not one specific incident that turned John from a top scholar to a "deadbeat" and "halfwit," rather it was a combination of events. Shotton wrote: "With our talent for accumulating black marks, John and I grew accustomed to being kept after school several days a week. When this failed to ameliorate our behavior, we were sent down for our first tête-à-tête with the [principal]."[20] It was the first of many visits the two would take to the headmaster's office.

John Lennon stands outside his aunt's house, which was called "Mendips."

A major part of John's problem, according to Shotton and other biographers, was the inability of the school's instructors to adapt their teaching to individual students. Everyone at Quarry Bank was forced to learn the same material in the same manner, whether that worked for the student or not. John's often-obscene art and writings—which those who saw them believed were excellent—were overlooked or ridiculed by his teachers, because they did not fit in with what others were doing. John did not let it discourage him. Art remained John's favorite subject, and he would draw whenever he could. Shotton said, "He'd do all these caricatures of the masters. We'd stick them on bits of cereal packets and make a stall at the school fete where people could throw darts at them."[21]

John later said it was about this time in his life that he began realizing he was different from other kids. He said:

> I used to think, I must be a genius, but nobody's noticed [*laugh*]. Either I'm a genius or I'm mad, which is it? "Well," I said. "I can't be mad because nobody's put me away; therefore I'm a genius." Genius is a form of madness and we're all that way. But I used to be a bit coy about it, like me guitar playing. If there's such a thing as genius— which is just *what*? . . . I am one. And if there isn't, I don't care. But I used to think it when I was a kid, writing me poetry and doing me paintings . . . I've been like this all me life. Genius is *pain* too. It's just pain.[22]

When his Uncle George suddenly died from a liver hemorrhage in 1955, John was profoundly impacted. Another father figure was gone from John's life, and this one was the only adult male confidant he ever had known. John's half sister said the death "came completely without warning. It was a terrible shock to us all, but especially to John who looked on him as a father. . . . George was his good friend, the ally on his side when things weren't going too well with Mimi."[23]

The death left John and his aunt Mimi home alone, save for the borders his aunt was forced to take in to help with the chores and pay the bills. Now fourteen, John began almost totally neglecting his studies and became a huge burden to his worried aunt. He also began to visit his mother more. As he grew into his teens, he found they had several things in common. He realized his mom was, in many ways, just a big kid, content on having fun and messing around. Her free spirit was the opposite of Aunt Mimi's strict demeanor. John's mother believed in living for the moment, and was not worried so much about the consequences of her actions. Having fun with life was her top priority.

Art remained John's favorite subject.

Pete Shotton often tagged along with John on his trips to his mother's house. Shotton said, "Her sense of the ridiculous was every bit as pronounced as John's. Sometimes, for instance, she would don a pair of spectacles with no glass in the frames; conversing with the neighbors or the postman, she'd nonchalantly push a finger through the nonexistent lens to rub her eyes."[24]

That type of mother-son tomfoolery was common when the pair were together. Humor helped form a bond between the two that time had not been able to. So did music. When John visited, his mother always was singing to the songs blasting out of the speakers wired from her record player into every room in her home. According to John's half sister, her mother and brother "sat up together after we were in bed chatting and listening to records. She was an ardent Elvis fan from the very beginning, and we grew up on a diet of his records, amongst others. . . . Sometimes we saw Mummy and John as they jived around the lounge to Elvis hits. 'Hound Dog,' 'Heartbreak Hotel,' 'Jailhouse Rock,' and 'Teddy Bear' were always played."[25]

"Rock & roll was real; everything else was unreal."

Elvis Presley had quickly become John's idol. He soaked up all the music he could get his hands on from the barely twenty-year-old Mississippi native. Though Presley's music was heavily influenced by the rhythm and blues black people had been playing for years, the sounds on his records were new to most white audiences, including most everyone in England. John even began imitating his newfound idol, wearing tight pants and sweeping his hair back from his forehead, all the while playing air guitar.

Discovering new music in the mid-1950s was nowhere near as easy as it is today. There was no turning on the computer to hear a thirty-second sample from an artist; no Web sites streaming low-quality, full-length tracks. Back then, there were only records and the radio, both which had huge impacts on John's life. The records came from John's mom and his pals. The radio came from Radio Luxembourg, a broadcast originating in Belgium that John used to religiously listen to late at night. The program was dedicated to playing the current American hit songs. To a fifteen-year-old creative English boy looking for an outlet for his rebellious tendencies, the sound coming through his speaker was a shot of pure heaven. The programming he had been able to hear on his country's popular BBC network had been unexciting and family oriented, not something that would appeal to an unruly teen. Of Radio Luxembourg, John said later, "That's the music that brought me from the provinces of England to the world. That's what made me what I am."[26]

The songs John was listening to were the beginnings of a musical style that would grow to dominate the charts, and it would regularly change the lives of those who listened to it. It was Bill Haley's "Rock Around the Clock," an up-tempo track filled with fast guitar licks, saxophone solos, and bluesy bass lines believed by many to be the first record that introduced rock and roll to a mainstream audience. It was Presley's cover of black blues singer Arthur Crudup's "That's All Right," and Buddy Holly's "That'll Be the Day." John was one person who believed rock and roll changed his life. He said, "[I]t was the only thing to get through to me after all the things that were happening to me when I was fifteen. Rock & roll was *real*; everything else was unreal."[27]

Although he may have looked the part of a rock and roller, John was a long ways from actually becoming one. He had been playing harmonica since he was in elementary school, and he had been known to have a decent musical ear, just as his mother and father had, but he never had performed on a serious level.

"The guitar's all very well, John. But you'll never make a living out of it."

All the musicians John listened to as a kid came from America, as no Englishmen at the time were playing rock and roll. But in 1956, that all changed. British musicians such as Tommy Steele began successfully copying the American stars, and some, most notably Lonnie Donegan, began making the style their own.

Donegan, a native of Glasgow, Scotland, pioneered a style of music called "skiffle, in which musicians used nontraditional instruments such as washboards, jugs, and other items to make their music. It was an adaptation of an American musical genre called "rockabilly." In his skiffle band, Donegan played acoustic guitar and sang, and his style of playing affected thousands of British kids once he became popular. His cover of black blues guitarist Leadbelly's

"Rock Island Line" debuted on the charts in 1956, and from there it was full steam ahead on the skiffle craze. Skiffle bands popped up across England, and Liverpool had more than its share of them. John wanted to start a skiffle band, too, but he had one minor problem: He did not play the guitar. He immediately set out to change that.

John called upon his mother, who still played banjo, and she taught John how to pick several of his favorite hit songs on that instrument. But what he really wanted was an acoustic guitar like Donegan and Presley played. John said, "I used to read the ads for guitars and just ache for one. Like everyone else, I used God for this one thing I wanted: 'Please God, give me a guitar.'"[28] After many days of prayer—and many more staring in the windows of stores and at the guitar ads in magazines—John's wish was granted.

The story of how John got his first guitar has varied through the years, depending on who was telling it. Some historians believe it was Aunt Mimi, who finally relented to her nephew's incessant begging. Others believe it was his mother, a theory supported by John's childhood friend, Pete Shotton, and Beatles biographer Hunter Davies. All report, however, that John's first guitar was a cheap, second-hand model. John did not seem to mind. He took a few lessons but did not like them, and learned some basic banjo chords from his mother, which he translated to the guitar as best he could. The first song he learned to play was "That'll Be the Day." John practiced relentlessly, much to the chagrin of Aunt Mimi, who wished her nephew would spend the time instead focusing on his studies. At one point, she even told him, "The guitar's all very well, John. But you'll never make a living out of it."[29]

The discouraging words did not faze him, and soon John formed his own band. John later said his of his first group, "I think the bloke whose idea it was didn't get in the group. We met in his house the first time. There was Eric Griffiths on guitar, Pete Shotton on washboard, Len Garry, Colin Hanton on drums and Rod [Davis] on banjo."[30] John sang and played guitar, just like Donegan and Presley. John's band members often changed depending on who was available and the band went through various names, too. The group of ambitious and inexperienced teenagers eventually began calling themselves the Quarrymen [sometimes written as two words, Quarry Men], after a line in the official song of Quarry Bank High School. The name stuck, and John had achieved his first major goal in life. He now had a band of his own.

Chapter 3

Becoming the Beatles

At their earliest performances, the Quarrymen's enthusiasm helped make up for their many musical shortcomings. John was the band's leader from the start, playing his cheap guitar with abandon, strumming so hard he often would break a string in the middle of a song, yet continue without missing a beat. No one even knew the proper way to play any songs, yet the band members faked their way through the hottest skiffle tracks from Lonnie Donegan and others, and also sprinkled in some good old American rock and roll.

John's playing and singing in these early shows, booked by the band's "manager" and friend, Nigel Whalley, stood out and those who were there have dubbed them memorable. But, like the thousands of other neighborhood skiffle acts that had popped up in Liverpool in the mid-1950s, it was almost certain that the Quarrymen would soon fade into obscurity. As with most musical fads, as skiffle clearly was, when the younger bands catch up, the fad has passed and some other style has taken hold. Occasionally, a band will evolve with the times and succeed, but the odds are stacked against most. On July 6, 1957, the odds of the Quarrymen being that one-in-a-million success story increased dramatically.

On that day, the Quarrymen were playing at a party at St. Peter's Parish Church in Woolton when John's childhood friend, Ivan Vaughan, brought a schoolmate of his to the show to introduce him to John. Ivan often brought people along to meet John. Sometimes, it was because he thought the two might have something in common. Other times, he thought the person had some shard of musical talent that could improve the Quarrymen. Ivan made his move at the end of the Quarrymen's first set, and introduced John to a baby-faced fifteen year old named Paul McCartney.

Paul McCartney

James Paul McCartney was born June 18, 1942, to working-class parents at Walton Hospital in Liverpool. His father, Jim, was a lathe turner at Napier's aircraft factory and his mother, Mary, was a nurse who once had worked at the hospital where Paul was born. His parents had waited a long time to marry and even longer to start a family. The pair wed just a year before James Paul—who became known by his middle name before he even came home from the hospital—was born, when Jim McCartney was thirty-nine years old and Mary

McCartney was thirty-two. Both were deep into their lives as singles when they met in June 1940.

Jim McCartney, an amateur musician with a good ear, was often seen pounding away to the current hit songs on the family piano. Years before Paul was born, Jim had been in a band called the Masked Melody Makers, and he had performed at small venues across Liverpool. His father's playing had a big impact on Paul, who later said, "My dad was actually a pretty fair pianist. . . . He played by ear, his left one! Actually he was deaf in one ear. He fell off a railing or something when he was a kid and busted an eardrum. . . . [H]e was definitely my strongest musical influence."[1]

Before Paul was two, his parents gave him his only sibling, Peter Michael, who also went by his middle name. Shortly after the family had grown to four, Jim McCartney lost his job, and his wife was forced to return to work. When Paul was four, his dad went back to work. Being a two-income family placed the McCartneys in a good spot financially, but by no means were they rich—or stable. The family was forced to move a lot to accommodate his father's job. When Paul began primary school, it was at Stockton Wood Road Primary in the small Liverpool suburb of Speke. He later transferred to the more-rural Joseph Williams Primary School in Belle Valle. He excelled at both institutions, and in 1953, was one of only four kids out of ninety who passed the eleven-plus exam, a requirement to enter a university. His score earned him a spot at the Liverpool Institute, one of the top schools in all of

The Quarrymen at their first concert at the Casbah Coffee House in 1959. Paul McCartney is on the left; John Lennon is on the right.

England. To get to the downtown Liverpool school, Paul had to ride the bus an hour each way.

Outside of school hours, the McCartney boys found much adventure in their rural setting. Their days often would begin—and end—with them playing on the banks of the Mersey River. Paul often would use these outdoor opportunities to practice for his stint in the military he was certain would come. He said, "I had to be prepared. In my mind I would imagine myself with a bayonet, running someone through, and I thought, Jesus Christ! That is not going to be easy. . . . What's the look on his face going to be like if I do it? So when I went out into the woods, I thought I'd better get some practice in."[2]

At fourteen, Paul's hour-long bus ride to school each day ended when the McCartneys moved closer to the center of Liverpool to a section of town called Allerton. That is where Paul's fascination with American rock and roll began, and also where he first heard Lonnie Donegan's skiffle music. Paul's studies began to suffer as his fascination with music and other art forms grew. He said, "I started to get interested in art instead of academic subjects. Then I started to see pictures of Elvis, and that started to pull me away from the academic path."[3] Though his parents had fancied him a doctor, that pull ultimately would prove too strong to fight.

Rock and roll music came into Paul's life around the same time his mother left it. Mary McCartney had long suffered from pains in her breast, and she had a mastectomy when breast cancer was discovered to be the cause. But by that point, the cancer was too far along, and Mary died of an embolism on October 31, 1956. The impact of her death was deep and immediate. Paul said, "I remember one horrible day me and my brother going to the hospital. They must have known she was dying. It turned out to be our last visit and it was terrible because there was blood on the sheets somewhere and seeing that, and your mother, it was like 'Holy cow!' . . . She was great. She was a really wonderful woman and really did pull the family along."[4]

Paul turned to music to cope with his mother's death, and he became obsessed with the art form.

Paul turned to music to cope with his mother's death, and he became obsessed with the art form. His discovery of rock and roll made the trumpet his father had given him passé, and now he wanted a guitar like his favorite musicians were playing. So he set out to get one. He said, "I went into town, swapped [the trumpet] in, got a guitar, came back home, couldn't figure out at all how to play it. I didn't realize that it was because I was left-handed. . . ."[5] Most guitars are geared for right-handed people, allowing them to strum the strings with their dominant hand. So Paul restrung the guitar backward allowing him to strum with his left hand. He played it nonstop, entered school talent shows, and learned the current hits. He even wrote songs, the first being "I Lost My Little Girl." He later said many people believed the song was about his mother, but he did not remember it being about her.

Paul was a fairly skilled musician by the time he was introduced to John Lennon, at least compared to most fifteen year olds. After the Quarrymen's performance had ended that summer day in 1956, he had the opportunity to show John how good he was. Hearing Paul playing and singing, John quickly realized this, though the egotistical leader in him also was a little intimidated by the younger boy. John remembered, "I thought, half to myself, 'He's as good as me.' I'd been kingpin up to then. Now I thought 'If I take him on, what will happen? . . . The decision was whether to keep me strong or make the group stronger. . . . It went through my head that I'd have to keep him in line if I let him join."[6]

Paul actually knew the proper chords to the songs he played, unlike John who only knew the banjo-translated versions. And Paul was singing the correct words, too. Soon, John's ego lost out to Paul's talent. John said, "[H]e was good, so he was worth having. He also looked like Elvis. I dug him."[7] Paul was asked to join the Quarrymen. He accepted, but was leaving on vacation for the rest of the summer, so he did not start practicing with them immediately. Paul's first show with the band was a dance at the New Clubmoor Hall in a prosperous section of Liverpool on October 18, 1957.

John and Paul dressed up for the show, donning cream-colored sport jackets, while the rest of the band wore white shirts with black ties. By all accounts,

Paul was less than spectacular during his debut with the Quarrymen. He made several mistakes, about which drummer Colin Hanton later said, "At first we were embarrassed, just really uncomfortable with what happened. John insisted on a certain degree of professionalism. And now the new guy made us look worse than the amateurs we were."[8] But Paul's flubs did not anger John, they actually made him laugh. A long-lasting and extremely successful partnership had begun.

By now, music had become the most-important aspect of John's life, a fact his aunt Mimi loathed. She wanted him to focus on his studies—or almost anything other than that blasted guitar—but John would not budge. So when he failed an important exam, which would have allowed him to continue on at Quarry Bank High School, Aunt Mimi stepped in to do something about it. Failing the test could have meant the end of John's formal education, and Mimi was having

The Quarrymen's lineup soon began to change.

none of it. Since John was talented at drawing, as well, Mimi demanded he apply to Liverpool College of Art. He had applied once before but had been rejected. But this time, with Mimi riding him the whole way, he was accepted into the school. For the next four years, studying at the downtown Liverpool school was to be John's full-time job.

Initially, school did shift some of John's focus from his music, but that did not last long. After Paul joined the Quarrymen, the two began spending a lot of time together practicing, playing, and eventually writing their own music. The Quarrymen's lineup soon began to change, with original members leaving and others coming on board. Over time, the quality of musicians in the band improved to the point that even John's best friend, Pete Shotton, was out of the band. His departure came after the two got into a drunken exchange at a party. Pete said, "John and I proceeded—for the first time in our lives—to get rip-roaring drunk. Toward the end of the evening, the two of us found ourselves sitting cross-legged on the floor with our instruments, surrounded by empty beer bottles."[9] After a while, Pete said John, "peremptorily seized my washboard and broke it over my head."[10] Pete, who said he had wanted to leave the band for a while anyway, was without an instrument, and without a spot in the Quarrymen. Ridding themselves of the washboard—and its not-so-talented player—helped move the Quarrymen further away from the skiffle sound and toward something that more closely resembled the American-style rock and roll John and Paul had long admired. The addition of a fourteen-year-old blue-chip guitarist continued moving the band in that direction.

George Harrison

Harry and Louise Harrison's fourth and final child was born too late to experience much of the poverty his three older siblings had to live through. By the time George Harold Harrison was born February 25, 1943, at his home in Liverpool, the Harrisons no longer had to rely on charity to help them get by. A couple of years prior, Harry Harrison had obtained a steady job as a bus driver, one which he kept for thirty-one years.

That did not mean the close-knit Harrisons were well-off. George's sister, Louise, said, "Mum made sure we knew we weren't peasants, that we came from educated stock and had great potential in life. She taught us how to think, to question things, to always be kind, never kowtow to big shots or lord over the lowly. . . . And we took care of one another. If there was only one apple, we'd each get a quarter."[11]

> **The big-eared, often-sick George was an entertainer from a young age.**

The big-eared, often-sick George was an entertainer from a young age. He regularly sang along with the tunes playing on his family's gramophone, and he entertained family and friends with his animal puppets. His sister said, "[H]e'd do skits with them for us. He was funny and outgoing and the family doted on him. He had fun growing up and was always the center of attention."[12]

When George was six, his family moved to a bigger house in Speke, the same Liverpool suburb the McCartney family called home. George enjoyed spending time in the area's natural surroundings, traveling by bicycle or foot to local lakes and ponds. He attended Dovedale Primary School, the same one John Lennon had, and was a decent student. Until he discovered his passion for music, that is.

It was 1953 by the time George's mother bought him his first guitar. It came from one of his classmates at Dovedale, and was a cheap, small-model instrument that was difficult to keep in tune. Its high-string action also made it difficult to play, especially for a ten year old with smallish hands. George's fingers bled regularly when he played, and he often became frustrated with his guitar. But he never stopped playing.

At twelve, George passed the eleven-plus exam, allowing him to enter the Liverpool Institute. The semi-exclusive school in the city's center did not turn out to be a good fit for George. Almost immediately, he began to rebel against his instructors, forsaking his studies due to a lack of interest. He skipped school to hang out and smoke cigarettes. His teachers were not able to capture his attention the way playing the guitar could. As was the case with many British teens of the time, it was rock and roll he longed to play, and Elvis Presley was his favorite. He and friend Arthur Kelly formed a short-lived skiffle band called the Rebels, with George's older brother, Pete, along for the ride playing a tea-chest bass, a rudimentary, deep-toned instrument made by attaching a stick and a string to the top of a wooden box, or chest.

George rode the same bus to the Institute as Paul McCartney did, and the two struck up a friendship centered on guitar playing and a love of rock and roll. They soon began practicing together, too, even as Paul

John Lennon in 1957 performing at a church function in Woolton, Great Britain.

was playing and practicing with the Quarrymen. When Paul first introduced George to John, the Quarrymen's leader was reluctant to let the much-younger kid join his band. That is until he saw him play in early 1958. Accounts differ as to exactly how and when George was officially allowed to join the Quarrymen, but most historians report that George's guitar playing was simply too good for John to deny. George later said John "was a bit embarrassed about [my age] because I was so tiny. I only looked about ten years old."[13] Actually, he was fourteen.

Even with the talented George on board, John and Paul remained front and center in each Quarrymen lineup. The pair spent hours practicing at each other's homes. John's art school was around the corner from the Liverpool Institute, so the two even got together for lunchtime jam sessions. Their personalities were as different as could be, but when they played music together, they somehow clicked. Paul said, "People always assume John was the hard-edged one and I was the soft-edged one, so much so that over the years I've come to accept that. . . . John, because of his upbringing and his unstable family life, had to be hard, witty, always ready for the cover-up, ready for the riposte, ready with the sharp little witticism. Whereas with my rather comfortable upbringing . . . my surface grew to be easy-going. . . . I think that was the balance between us. . . ."[14]

John and Paul wrote several early songs together. Some, including "One After 909" and "Love Me Do," were good enough to surface on future recordings. The pair came to an early agreement. Regardless of who had written which part, the team of "Lennon-McCartney" always would be listed as the song's writers. Though that was not the case in mid-1958, when the Quarrymen recorded for the first time in the home of a man named Percy Phillips. With little money to pay for their recording, the Quarrymen were forced to record their chosen two songs in one take each. They chose Buddy Holly's "That'll Be the Day" as their main song on the record, or the A-side, while the other song, or B-side, was an original tune called "In Spite of All the Danger." When they were done recording, Phillips pressed the music as the band—which now included Lennon, McCartney, Harrison, Colin Stanton, and piano player John "Duff" Lowe—waited. The final product was a flimsy record—though both songs were well done, especially given the circumstance—with song titles handwritten on it by Phillips. Both sides of the disk read "Recorded by P. F. Phillips," and listed the composers of the respective songs. For "In Spite of All the Danger," on which Lennon sang lead vocals, that credit was given to the team of "McCartney, Harrison." The record later became the most-sought-after record ever produced, worth an estimated two hundred thousand dollars.

> **John and Paul became friends as well as musical partners.**

John and Paul became friends as well as musical partners, although neither of their families approved of their relationship, and they discouraged them from hanging out. The only family member who did not seem to mind the pair hanging out was John's mother, Julia. In fact, she encouraged it, and even told them what current hits she thought they should learn. Unfortunately, Julia never got to see the heights her son's songwriting partnership eventually would take him to.

With darkness closing in on the warm summer evening of July 15, 1958, Julia decided it was time to end her visit at Aunt Mimi's house to return home, where John was waiting to see her. As Julia was about to leave, Nigel Whalley showed up looking for his buddy, John. When he found he was not there, Nigel offered to walk Julia to her bus stop. When they got there, Nigel turned to head to his own home as Julia crossed Menlove Avenue. She was more than halfway to her destination when Nigel heard the sound of screeching tires. Turning to face the sound, Nigel saw Julia's body fly through the air and crash to the ground, where he rushed to be by her side. Mimi had heard the accident from inside her house and ran outside to attend to her sister. An ambulance arrived a few minutes later and took Julia to the hospital, but it was no use. John's mother was dead. She was only forty-four years old.

Across town, John had noticed his mother was later than usual, but he was not prepared for the news he received when he answered a knock on her door. John said, "An hour or so after it happened a copper came to the door to let us know about the accident. It was awful, like some dreadful film where they ask you if you're the victim's son and all that. Well, I was, and I can tell you it was absolutely the worst night of my entire life."[15]

John was devastated. His mother's death dealt a big behavioral setback to the already-unruly seventeen-year-old. He did not mention it often, but when he did, he told of the impact it had on his life. He said, "I lost my mother twice. Once as a child of five and then again at seventeen. It made me very, very bitter inside. I had just begun to re-establish a relationship with her when she was killed. We'd caught up on so much in just a few short years. We could communicate. We got on. Deep down inside, I thought, 'Sod it! I've no real responsibilities to anyone now.'"[16]

John's half sisters, Julia and Jacqui, were asleep when the police officer showed up at their house. Julia, eleven at the time, only remembers "the most horrible sound coming from our parents' room next door. It was our father crying, dreadful, racking sobs alternated with moans. It was very frightening."[17] The girls eventually were lied to, and they were told that their mother was in the hospital. They were taken to Scotland to live with their aunt and uncle. They were not allowed to attend the funeral, nor did they even know one was taking place. In fact, they were not told of their mother's death for several weeks after it had occurred.

For John, the period following his mother's death was filled with self-destruction. Though he had dabbled with alcohol before, he now began drinking regularly and acting out more than ever. He never was a great student, but now he all but gave up on his studies. He even began dressing the part of what was known as a Teddy boy, rebelling against authority with his long jacket, suede shoes, skinny tie, and greased-back hair.

Paul said, "The image was a protective measure. . . . He wore big long [sideburns] and so we looked up to him as a sort of violent Teddy boy. . . . At art college he was considered to be a bit of a hot-head. He got drunk a lot and once he kicked the telephone box in, which got him a reputation."[18]

Even the Quarrymen's public appearances—which recently had grown to be quite frequent—declined after the death of John's mother. But John did turn to the guitar for comfort, and continued composing songs with Paul, with whom he now shared a morbid connection. Paul said, "Now we were both in this; both losing our mothers. This was a bond for us, something of ours, a special thing. We'd both gone through that trauma and both came out the other side and we could actually laugh about it in the sick humour of the day."[19] Years later, John sang "a song of love" for his mom on the track "Julia," which was released in 1968. Two years later, he told his mom "good-bye" in the song "Mother."

"I lost my mother twice. Once as a child of five and then again at seventeen. It made me very, very bitter inside."

Although his school days were numbered, John still hung out around the Liverpool College of Art, mostly so he could socialize. He had his first serious girlfriend a couple years earlier—a curvy, blonde neighborhood girl named Barbara Baker—but art school is where John's love life fully bloomed. His first college girlfriend was Thelma Pickles, with whom he had a short, often-heated relationship. She said John, still reeling from his mom's death, would lash out in anger. She said, "He could be very unbearable at times. He was never violent . . . but he would say things to hurt you. I think it was a defense thing, because he could be vulnerable at times [like] when you talked about his mother. He would become almost dreamy and very quiet."[20] Thelma's replacement on John's arm was a fellow art school student named Cynthia Powell.

> "When I'd first looked at John I'd thought, yuck, not my type."

Powell was a year older than Lennon, but the two immediately clicked. Like Lennon, she also had lost a parent when she was young—her dad had died of lung cancer when she was seventeen. She and John met in lettering class. It certainly was not love at first sight, at least not for Powell, who said, "When I'd first looked at John I'd thought, yuck, not my type. With his Teddy-boy look—DA (duck's arse) haircut, narrow drainpipe trousers and a battered old coat that was too big for him—he was very different from the clean-cut boys I was used to. His outspoken comments and caustic wit were alarming: I was terrified he might turn on me, and he soon did, calling me 'Miss Prim' or 'Miss Powell' and taking the mickey out of my smart clothes and posh accent."[21]

But Powell soon softened, and she began falling for Lennon once he began showing her more of his sensitive side. He even serenaded her one afternoon with a song he had written called, "Ain't She Sweet." Powell said, "Halfway through the term I realized I was falling for him and scolded myself. I was being ridiculous; he wasn't at all the type of boy I'd imagined myself with and, in any case, I couldn't see him being interested in me."[22] She even changed her hairstyle and the way she dressed to attract his attention. It turns out she did not have to work so hard. One night after a holiday party, Lennon told her he had had a crush on her the whole year. The two began dating, and Cynthia would grow to play an important role in Lennon's life. So would another person he met in art school. This one was a talented artist named Stuart Sutcliffe.

Stuart Sutcliffe

Born June 23, 1940, in Edinburgh, Scotland, Stuart Fergusson Victor Sutcliffe—like many children born during World War II—was a military child. His father, Charles, was a naval officer frequently away at sea, and his mother, Millie, was a school teacher. When he was three, his family moved to Liverpool, where Stuart began carving a name for himself as an artist. That led to him being accepted into the Liverpool College of Art at the young age of sixteen.

Though he and Lennon were the same age, Sutcliffe was a year ahead in school, and much more respected as an artist. Beatles biographer Bob Spitz describes

Sutcliffe as being "far and away the most talented student in the place, gifted with a seemingly effortless mastery of every medium he touched, drawing, painting, or sculpture. He was also phenomenally energetic, filling canvases and sketchbooks with work of a maturity that dazzled his instructors. . . ."[23] It also dazzled Lennon, who already had heard of Sutcliffe before the pair were formally introduced by a mutual friend.

Sutcliffe's musical ability was as poor as his artistic ability was good, but he loved rock and roll nearly as much as Lennon. The two bonded over songs and art, and formed a deep friendship that arguably became the best Lennon would ever have. Sutcliffe's sister, Pauline, said, "John had a desperate quest for a certain kind of nurturing. Stuart's nurturing was unconditional. . . . He loved him. And John recognized that Stuart believed in him . . . that he believed he wasn't just a mad, destructive anarchist, but was somebody of worth. Stuart freed John's own creative spirit."[24]

The accuracy of Pauline Sutcliffe's assessment is impossible to determine, although Lennon did appear to care for his diminutive friend. By late 1959, The Quarrymen had dwindled down to just the three guitarists: Lennon, McCartney, and Harrison. The trio briefly flirted with a name change to Johnny and the Moondogs for an audition for a spot on *The Carol Levis Discovery* television show (which they did not win), but quickly realized they needed a drummer and a bassist if they were to keep pace with the current rock and roll outfits. The bass player's spot was filled in November, after Sutcliffe sold one of his paintings at an art show and used the money to buy a bass guitar. He had no experience with the instrument, but Lennon welcomed him into his group, regardless.

The band still was without a drummer, thanks to the unpleasant departure of Colin Hanton a short time earlier. Hanton said, "I left the Quarrymen after playing a booking at the Pavilion Theatre in Lodge Lane. We had drunk a few beers during the interval and an argument started on the way home on the bus. I got off to catch another bus to take me home to Woolton and somehow or other that was that, they never contacted me again to ask me to play. I saw John a few times and he told me that they had got a drummer called Pete, which must have been Pete Best."[25]

Best did eventually take the Quarrymen's drum chair, but first the band went through a few short-time replacements, including Tommy Moore, who was in his mid-thirties when he joined the group. In August 1960, Best finally came on to drum with Lennon, McCartney, Harrison, and Sutcliffe.

> **Sutcliffe's musical ability was as poor as his artistic ability was good, but he loved rock and roll nearly as much as Lennon.**

Pete Best

Randolph Peter Best's background was more diverse—and his family better off financially—than all the other

55

The Casbah as it looks today.

Quarrymen. Pete, as his family called him, was born November 24, 1941, in India, where his once-successful boxing promoter father, John Best, was stationed as a physical education teacher for the British army. Pete's mother, Mona, was a Red Cross worker also living in India, which is where the couple had met.

When World War II ended in 1945, the Best family left for Britain, ending up in Liverpool, where Pete began attending school. In his autobiography, *Beatle! The Pete Best Story,* Pete writes that he "went to various schools until I won a scholarship to Liverpool Collegiate in Shaw Street. By my mid-teens I had . . . decided that perhaps the teaching profession was the one for me. I suppose you would describe us as a middle-class family and teaching somehow fit into that pattern. That is, until the Casbah came along."[26]

The Casbah did alter the course of Pete's life, and the lives of countless other Liverpudlians coming of age in the late-1950s. The Casbah was a rudimentary club located in the expansive cellar of the Best family home. Starting it had been Pete's mother's idea. She said, "My home was beginning to resemble a railway station . . . there was always someone passing through. My original idea had been to start a little exclusive club for Peter and his friends . . . and thus put an end all this trooping in and out of the living quarters."[27]

If Mona Best needed any validation that her idea was a good one, she quickly got it. Soon, there were hundreds of teenagers wanting to join the club, and after a major remodel of the cellar, it opened up to the general public. The Quarrymen were the first to play there, on August 29, 1959. They played the club several more times, and the Casbah's membership grew as time went on. The club also became a regular hangout for Lennon and the other band members, even when they were not playing.

Living at the club left Pete constantly around musicians, and he soon began to tinker on the drums. His tinkering evolved into a stint with his first band, The Blackjacks. As Pete's skills progressed, and Lennon and Co. had begun yet another search for a permanent drummer, Pete was invited to tryout. He wrote in his autobiography: "We played for about twenty minutes in all and at the end they all reached the same conclusion: 'Yeh! You're in, Pete!'"[28]

After all the personnel changes, and the shift in the band's musical style from skiffle to mostly rock and roll, the name Quarrymen no longer seemed to fit. Lennon decided it was time for a new name for his band. After a few name changes, the band went with The Silver Beetles then dropped the first word, added an "a" where the second "e" would be, and became the Beatles.

Chapter 4

Made in Germany

The stories behind the genesis of the Beatles' name are numerous, and they range from the reasonable to the absurd. The most-common belief is that Sutcliffe came up with the name. Beatles biographer Hunter Davies wrote in his book *The Beatles* about the difficulties of determining the name's origin. He wrote:

> It had come from that Marlon Brando film, *The Wild One*. There is a group of motorcyclists in the film, all in black leather, called the Beetles, though they are only referred to as such in passing. Stu Stucliffe saw this film, heard the remark, and came back and suggested it to John as the new name for their group. John said yeh, but we'll spell it Beatles, as we're a beat group. Well, that's one theory. No doubt, in years to come, there will be new suggestions.[1]

Davies's story has been echoed by several sources close to the band at the time, although new suggestions have arisen. At various times, Lennon even took credit for coming up with the name, and Harrison also has contradicted the story he told Davies, and given Lennon credit a time or two. Another common theory is that the name was inspired by the name of Buddy Holly's band, the Crickets.

Best joined the band shortly after the other four members had returned from a somewhat disastrous tour of Scotland in support of Liverpool native, and Elvis Presley lookalike, Johnny Gentle. Best was almost immediately thrown into the fire. Within a few weeks, he and the rest of the Beatles set off for Hamburg, Germany, for a forty-eight-night residency at the Indra Club. It was a trip that would shape their careers—and lives—for years to come.

When the Beatles arrived in Hamburg in the middle of August 1960, the five young lads discovered that the city was much like their home base of Liverpool. Both were gritty port cities—Hamburg on the Elbe River, Liverpool on the Mersey. Both had been hit hard by enemy bombs during the war, and now they had their share of crime and illicit underground activity. Even so, Hamburg's reputation was by far the worst of the two. The Beatles were thrust right into the city's seedy side. The small Indra Club was located inside the basement of a former strip club smack in the middle of the Hamburg's red-light district, where prostitution and gang combat was commonplace. But Allan Williams, the Liverpool club owner and de facto Beatles manager responsible for booking the band in Hamburg, had been told the city was a great place for bands to play.

Williams eventually would be proven correct, but not at first.

In fact, just a handful of people witnessed the first Beatles show at Indra, and those who did were not impressed. The cramped stage the band was sharing used to be where the strippers would dance, and the Germans that frequented the club were used to seeing serious movement from the performers on the stage. The Beatles were a fairly tame bunch when performing. They did not jump around wildly; instead they would rather calmly sing their songs and play their instruments. This was not working for the Indra Club regulars. On subsequent nights, they began chanting *Mach Schau* [make show] to the band, signaling they wanted to see some energy. John said, "So we tried. We were a bit scared by it all at first, being in the middle of the tough club land. But we felt cocky, being from Liverpool, at least believing the myth about Liverpool producing cocky people."[2]

John described his first attempt at "making show" to biographer Hunter Davies. He said he would "jump around in one number like Gene Vincent. Every number lasted twenty minutes, just to spin it out. We all [made show] all the time from then."[3] Davies writes that John "made show all the time, jumping in ecstasy

When the Beatles arrived in Hamburg in the middle of August 1960, the five young lads discovered that the city was much like their home base of Liverpool.

or rolling on the floor, much to the amusement of the local rockers they were soon getting as their fans. Stories about John are still told in Hamburg, a lot of them improving with age."[4] As soon as Lennon and the rest of the Beatles began to *Mach Schau*, the crowds slowly began to grow.

The Beatles' life in Hamburg was far from glamorous. They had to play four and a half hours each night, and six hours on weekends. They played from early in the evening until early the following morning, sometimes seven days a week. The workload forced the band to come up with new material to fill the hours, and they also had to lengthen the songs they already had. It was on-the-job training with the pay coming both in money and beer, which the crowd would literally hand the band members as they performed.

Off stage, the Beatles were housed in cramped quarters in the Bambi Kino, a run-down theater owned by the owner of the Indra Club, Bruno Koschmider. Their accommodations there were far worse than any of them could have imagined prior to arriving in Germany. The quintet lived in three small dressing rooms behind the theater's screen, and they used the urinals for both their intended purpose and to wash themselves.

Hamburg was a city where sexuality was openly talked about and sex acts were openly performed. It was a far cry from Liverpool's more-conservative attitude on the topic, and girls began flocking to the Beatles. This certainly must have worried Cynthia Powell, John's longtime girlfriend who was back in Liverpool as her

The Quarrymen in the early 1960s in Germany. From left to right: Pete Best, George Harrison, John Lennon, Paul McCartney, and Stuart Sutcliffe.

nineteen-year-old steady received numerous propositions from Hamburg's sexually desensitized women. Powell said, "I wrote to John, enclosing what I hoped were sexy photographs, taken in the Woolworth's photo booth—the latest in new technology. I was determined to do what I could to keep him faithful, so I would put on my most provocative outfit and pout as seductively as I knew how."[5]

Despite of what he was—or wasn't—doing with other women, Lennon continued to write Powell back. She said, "He wrote to me almost every day, letters that were ten pages long, covered with kisses, cartoons and declarations of love. Even the envelopes bore poems, kisses and messages like 'Postman, Postman, don't be slow, I'm in love with Cyn so go, man go.'"[6]

After numerous noise complaints from someone living above the Indra, Koschmider decided to revert the basement space to a strip club, and he moved the Beatles down the street to the nicer Kaiserkeller club, where they opened for another Liverpool band, Rory Storm and The Hurricanes. Kaiserkeller is where Klaus Voorman first discovered the Beatles, as did his longtime girlfriend, Astrid Kirchherr.

One night as he was walking by the Kaiserkeller, Voorman poked his head into the club to see who was creating the brilliant sounds he could hear from the streets. A few nights later, he and Kirchherr returned to the club. It was a move the young German man would soon regret. The good-looking Kirchherr took an immediate liking to the Beatles—both to their music and to the individuals producing it. Her favorite Beatle was Sutcliffe, and she and the artist-turned-bass player quickly struck up a romantic relationship, leaving Voorman without a girlfriend.

Spending time with Sutcliffe also meant spending time with the other members of the Beatles, and Kirchherr had a big impact on all of them. She trimmed their hair into a style closely resembling her own—a forward-combed, bowl-shaped style that the Beatles eventually would become famous for. The twenty-two-year-old Kirchherr, along with her friend Jurgen Vollmer, also photographed the band several times, the first photographer to do so seriously. She said, "I did big prints showing their expressions naturally, not asking them to pose, and they went crazy. They'd never seen anything like these in their lives."[7]

> "Postman, Postman, don't be slow, I'm in love with Cyn so go, man go."

Hamburg also was where the Beatles were introduced to something else they had not seen before, the stimulant Preludin, better known as prellies, which was prescribed for weight loss, but also taken for the energy its users received. Prellies became a late-night staple in all the Beatles' diets, helping them maintain their vigor and stay awake, even after a long, hard night playing music in a sweaty club. Lennon proved to be particularly vulnerable to the drug. Kirchherr said the prellies allowed him to "open up about himself,"[8] but the commonly held belief that the Beatles were always on drugs when they were in Hamburg was not true. She said:

> Drugs? It was just a big laugh. The stories that the Beatles were all doped up during their visits to Hamburg is so much rubbish. We were young kids. George, particularly, was a baby of seventeen. We could only afford to drink beer, which was the cheapest, and then one of us discovered these little pills called Preludin. . . . We discovered that when you took them and drank beer, you felt great. You didn't get drunk but you got all speedy and talked away like mad. . . . We had maybe one and a half for the whole night.[9]

McCartney said he was so wired naturally, that he often passed on the prellies, "Or I'd maybe have one pill, while the guys, John particularly, would have four or five during the course of an evening and get totally wired. I always felt I could have one and get as wired as they got just on the conversation."[10]

Their stay in Hamburg extended thanks to their success, the Beatles were offered the chance to move from the Kaiserkeller to the new Top Ten Club in late October. But soon the police were tipped off to the fact that George Harrison was only seventeen, and he had no working permit that would allow him to legally be in Germany. He was not even old enough to be in the clubs he had been playing in since August. George was given twenty-four hours to leave the country, and he had to take a train back to Liverpool.

The day after George left, a mischievous McCartney and Best set a small fire at the Bambi Kino. Though it did no damage, the two were arrested for attempted arson, and they were also found to have no working permits to be in Germany and were deported back to England. Defeated and now without bandmates, Lennon returned to England on his own, while Sutcliffe—who now was engaged to be married to Kirchherr—stayed behind in Hamburg.

Lennon arrived back at Mendips in the middle of the night, dejected, defeated, and depressed. The house was shuttered for the evening, and Lennon had to throw rocks at Aunt Mimi's window to wake her. Mimi, who had warned her nephew against going to Germany at the expense of his studies, was not kind. She wanted to know where all the money was he had told her he was going to make. She said, "He had these awful cowboy boots on, up to [his knees] they were, all gold and silver. He just pushed past me and said, 'Pay that taxi, Mimi.' I shouted after him up the stairs, 'Where's your [one-hundred pounds] a week, John?'"[11] Lennon shouted back, "Just like you, Mimi, to go on about [money] when you know I'm tired."[12] Then he headed up to his old room above the front porch. For a while before he left for Germany, Lennon had been sharing an apartment with Sutcliffe near Liverpool Art College. But now, feeling defeated, he was back at Mendips, under the watchful eye of his strict aunt.

> **Defeated and now without bandmates, Lennon returned to England on his own.**

67

Lennon laid low for a while after his return. Some accounts say he did not leave Mendips for more than a week. Cynthia Powell said Lennon was excited to see her, that he called as soon as he returned, and he took her to buy a leather jacket with the money he had made in Hamburg. Whatever he did, Lennon did not see any of the other Beatles for a couple weeks, and he often thought about how the band might be finished. For a period, it looked like that might be the case. In the time Lennon was spending sulking, a couple of the Beatles had gotten jobs, including Harrison, who thought his bandmates were still playing in Germany.

The first comeback show happened December 17 at the Casbah.

Of course, they were not, but it would not be long before they reformed again and started playing in Liverpool. The first comeback show happened December 17 at the Casbah. Show posters advertising the gig were plastered across town. With Sutcliffe still in Hamburg, Chas Newby, a member of Pete Best's former group, The Blackjacks, played bass. Ten days later, a disc jockey named Bob Wooler helped the Beatles get another gig at the Litherland Town Hall. The crowd there hardly knew of the Beatles, but from the opening riff of the first song, Little Richard's raucous "Long Tall Sally," the crowd was mesmerized. Instead of socializing in their own little groups as they did for most bands, the club-goers rushed to the stage to feed off the energy the

The Beatles, circa 1960. From left to right: Paul McCartney, Pete Best, Stuart Sutcliffe, George Harrison, and John Lennon.

band members were exuding with their own dancing and head-bobbing.

Beatles scholars have since recognized that night, December 27, 1960, as a major turning point in the career of the band. From there, it was all uphill. Lennon said, "It was that evening that we really came out of our shell and let go. We discovered we were quite famous. It was when we began to think for the first time that we were good. Up to Hamburg we'd thought we were OK, but not good enough."[13]

Music promoter Brian Kelly agreed with Lennon, and said of the Litherland show, "I was completely knocked out by them. They had a pounding, pulsating beat which I knew would be big at the box office. When they had finished playing I posted some bouncers on the door of their dressing room to prevent some other promoters, who were in the hall, entering. I went inside and booked them solidly for months ahead."[14]

With the assistance of Kelly and other promoters, the Beatles—with Stuart Sutcliffe now back from Germany and on bass—began playing out in many other Liverpool clubs. At Litherland, they were billed every Thursday as "The Magnificent Beatles!! John, Paul, George and Pete."[15] Sutcliffe was not mentioned.

The Beatles also played at the Cavern Club, the jazz club where the Quarrymen had once played to little success. But musical trends had changed since that time, and the old warehouse was now a happening rock and roll hangout soon to become the Beatles' home away from home. During the next two years, the band played there nearly three hundred times. Many of those shows came during lunchtime, when Lennon should have been in school. That is, if he still were enrolled. But Lennon had stopped attending art college prior to his first trip to Germany, and he was never to go back.

Beatles' songs would often energize the crowd that fights would break out. Sutcliffe was badly beaten during one on January 30, 1961. As he was loading equipment after a show at Lathom Hall in Liverpool, he was attacked by a group of men, who kicked and punched him so many times that he was a bloody mess by the time someone else showed up to fight off the bullies. At various times, other band members were beaten up, as well, and sometimes they would even fight one another. A few months after he was first beaten, Sutcliffe was whipped until he bled by the man he most admired, John Lennon. Lennon, drunk at the time, was upset over some band-related issues and took it out on Sutcliffe. Lennon's frustrations with Sutcliffe's place in the band were shared by McCartney and Harrison. Both men had been pressuring Lennon to toss his friend out, both because his musical ability—as Sutcliffe himself was well aware—was not up to par with the other members, and also because his focus was shifting from music back to painting.

Sutcliffe's altercation with Lennon occurred in Hamburg, where the Beatles had returned in April 1961 for another tour. Sutcliffe quit the band while they were there, leaving the Beatles in a desperate situation. Who was going to play bass, the least-appealing instrument of all? Lennon and Harrison refused to give up their guitars, so Paul agreed to. He bought a violin-shaped bass and took over Sutcliffe's four-string duties. Paul said, "Nobody wants to play bass, or nobody did in those days. Bass was the thing that the fat boys got lumbered with and were asked to stand at the back and play. . . . So I definitely didn't want to do it but Stuart left, and I got lumbered with it. Later I was quite happy, I enjoyed it. . . ."[16]

> "Once upon a time there were three little boys called John, George and Paul. . . . All of a sudden they grew guitars and learned a noise."

In June, the Beatles were asked to perform as the backup band for singer Tony Sheridan at a recording session held at a local school. They agreed to, and they recorded seven songs. One of them, "My Bonnie," was released as a single later that year on Polydor Records, and it did mildly well on the German charts, where it was released as coming from Sheridan and "The Beat Brothers," which the producer had insisted the Beatles be called. That producer, popular German musician Bert Kaempfert, was impressed by "The Beat Brothers," and signed them to a one-year contract with Polydor. Kaempfert also allowed the Beatles to record two of their own songs that day, an instrumental called "Cry for a Shadow," and a version of the jazz song "Ain't She Sweet," featuring Lennon on lead vocals. Neither of those songs was released, but the recording session did go down in history as being the Beatles' first.

72

When they returned to England in July, the Beatles resumed their performances at the Cavern Club. That month also saw the launch of *Mersey Beat*, a local newspaper focusing on the Liverpool music scene. The publication was founded by Bill Harry, a friend of Lennon's from Liverpool Art College. Harry allowed Lennon to write an article on the history of the Beatles for the paper's first edition. It ran July 6, 1961, under the headline: "BEING A SHORT DIVERSION ON THE DUBIOUS ORIGINS OF BEATLES." Lennon's writing, which ran on the front page, provided a tongue-in-cheek biographical sketch of the band. It began:

> Once upon a time there were three little boys called John, George and Paul, by name christened. They decided to get together because they were the getting together type. When they were together they wondered what for after all, what for? All of a sudden they all grew guitars and learned a noise. Funnily enough, no one was interested, least of all the three little men. So on discovering a fourth little even littler man called Stuart Sutcliffe running about them they said, quote "Sonny get a bass guitar and you will be alright" and he did— but he wasn't alright because he couldn't play it. So they sat on him with comfort 'til he could play. Still there was no beat, and a kindly old aged man said, quote "Thou hast not drums!" We had no drums! they coffed. So a series of drums came and went and came.[17]

Mersey Beat became highly popular in Liverpool, and it featured several more articles on the Beatles, including one announcing that they had signed a recording contract with Polydor. The newspapers were sold across the city, including at the North End Music Stores, or NEMS, run by twenty-seven-year-old Brian Epstein. Born into a well-off Jewish family, Epstein began his work career managing a small record section in his family's furniture stores. Shortly after *Mersey Beat* began, Epstein began contributing a column to each issue, focusing on new releases at his record store.

Though "My Bonnie" had done nothing on the English charts, people still came into Epstein's shop looking for a copy of it. Epstein said that is how he came to hear about the Beatles, and legend says a record buyer named Raymond Jones was the one who asked for it. Epstein wrote in his autobiography, "The name 'Beatle' meant nothing to me. . . . I had never [before] given a thought to any of the Liverpool beat groups then up and coming in the cellar clubs."[18] Some Beatle historians doubt Epstein's story, saying he surely must have at least heard about the Beatles prior to Jones's trip to his store. Especially considering all the coverage the band was receiving in *Mersey Beat* and the airplay "My Bonnie" was beginning to get on Liverpool radio.

Regardless of how he came to learn of the band, Epstein decided it was time for him to see for himself what all the hoopla surrounding the Beatles was about. On November 9, 1961, the sharp-dressed businessman showed up at the Cavern Club and stuck his nose in the door. That move shaped the Beatles' career, and in turn, the future of the entire music industry. Epstein said:

John Lennon in the Cavern Club in
Liverpool in the early 1960s.

It was pretty much an eye-opener, to go down into this darkened, dank, smoky cellar in the middle of the day, and to see crowds and crowds of kids watching these four young men on stage. They were rather scruffily dressed, in the nicest possible way, or, I should say, in the most attractive way: black leather jackets and jeans, long hair of course. . . . I immediately liked what I heard. They were fresh and they were honest, and they had what I thought was a sort of presence and, this is a terribly vague term, star quality.[19]

Epstein watched the band several more times before inviting them to his office in December. That is when he offered to be their manager. The band had their concerns, most notably, would they still be able to play the same music? Epstein assured them they would. The band agreed to let Epstein manage them, and he immediately set to work on his new task. He cleaned up their image and turned them into professional musicians, stressing punctuality—which they never had been good at—and focusing their attention on the music.

Almost immediately, Epstein set off to get the Beatles out of their contract with Polydor, which he did, and find the band a new recording contract. On the first day of 1962, he had the boys in London at an audition for Decca Records. The tryout was long, and did not work out for the Beatles. Decca passed on giving them a record deal. The Decca rejection was not the only one the Beatles would face, but Epstein remained determined. He believed he was onto something, and continued his search for a deal.

Meanwhile, Epstein sent the Beatles back to Germany to play a series of shows at Hamburg's new Star-Club. Rather than cram into a van with several other people, as they had on their previous trips to Germany, the Beatles flew this go-round. The band—minus Harrison, who came a day later—arrived at the Hamburg airport on April 11, and were greeted there by their friend Astrid Kirchherr. Lennon was happy to see her, but there was no smile on the young woman's face and her voice was missing the power he always had known her to possess. He knew something was wrong. Kirchherr said, "Stuart's died, John. He's gone."[20]

Lennon reacted in a manner that may sound strange to most: He burst out with laughter. Kirchherr said, "It was frightening. John was laughing but also kind of crying, saying 'No, no, no!' and lashing out with his hands."[21] Lennon's seemingly insensitive display was not out of character, nor did it mean he did not care for Sutcliffe. Many historians have written about how Lennon loved the twenty-one-year-old Sutcliffe like a brother. For evidence, they point to the fact that when Sutcliffe had remained behind in Germany, effectively ending his stint with the Beatles, Lennon began hand-writing him letters filled with heartfelt poetry, drawings, and soul-bearing words. Kirchherr believes Lennon's reaction to the news of Sutcliffe's death was "his way of not wanting to face the truth. John went deep into himself for just a little while after the news. But he and I didn't speak much

> **"Stuart's died, John. He's gone."**

about Stuart. I knew that he and Stuart genuinely loved each other. They told me so, when they got loose."[22]

Sutcliffe had died April 10, a day before the Beatles entered the country. He had been having terrible headaches for months, and officially died from a "cerebral hemorrhage due to bleeding into the right ventricle of the brain."[23] An autopsy revealed a small indentation in the front of Sutcliffe's skull, which likely had been caused by a major blow to the head. Exactly what that blow was will never be known, but one theory is that it happened during the beating he had taken more than a year earlier outside Lathom Hall. Some historians have even suggested that the damage to Sutcliffe's skull could have been caused by the beating Lennon had given him in Hamburg. Exactly where the truth lies, no one will ever know.

The distraught band members pulled themselves together after hearing of Sutcliffe's death, and they decided to carry on with their shows.

The distraught band members pulled themselves together after hearing of Sutcliffe's death, and they decided to carry on with their shows. And like most of the Beatles' gigs in Hamburg, they were wild ones. The now-legendary stories from that tour include one where a drunken Lennon took the stage with a toilet seat around his neck, several fighting stories, and another incident where Lennon urinated over the edge of a hotel balcony.

McCartney said, "We were just normal human beings. I seem to remember John had a pee over the edge. But what happens is that all these stories grow into great legends."[24]

At the time, the stories were nowhere near legendary, because no one outside of a few select areas cared—or even had heard—of John Lennon, Paul McCartney, George Harrison, Pete Best, or their band. Shortly after the band's third trip to Hamburg, that all changed forever.

Chapter 5

Beatlemania

Spreads

Brian Epstein left the band by themselves in Hamburg, choosing instead to stay in England to continue his search for a record deal. His hope was dwindling fast. He still believed in the band's potential, but he also had spent a lot of his own money promoting them, and he appeared ready to give up. With the band's music in his hand, he took a trip to London to give it one final shot. Oddly, it was a trip to a record store there that helped change his fortunes.

Epstein stopped by the store to make some more copies of the demos he was hawking. One of the store's employees liked the recordings, and hooked Epstein up with a friend of his at Parlophone Records, a subsidiary of the gigantic EMI corporation. That friend, George Martin, was head of Parlophone and agreed to give the Beatles an audition. An excited Epstein sent a telegram to the band in Hamburg. It read, "Congratulations boys,

EMI requests recording session. Please rehearse new material."[1]

That audition took place June 6, 1962, at EMI's Abbey Road Studios in London. Just as the telegraph had told them to, the band did rehearse their new material and played it for Martin. Four songs were recorded that day, including the three originals, "Ask Me Why," "Love Me Do," and "P.S. I Love You." Martin appeared to be impressed by both the songs and the band members. Everyone that is, except Pete Best. Martin felt his drumming was not up to par with what the rest of the band was producing. After the tryout, Martin took Epstein aside and told him Best would have to go. For the time being, Epstein kept Martin's message to himself.

In his autobiography, Best said he soon got wind that something might be up with his status in the band. He then confronted Epstein, who said, "I'm telling you as manager, there are no plans to replace you, Pete."[2] Best said he still had not been told when Martin decided to sign the Beatles that July. Best said that it was not until August that he was called into a meeting in Epstein's office. The band's manger told him that the other band members wanted him to be replaced because they—and more importantly, Martin—did not think he was a good enough drummer. Best later wrote: "I was stunned and found words difficult. Only one echoed through my mind. Why, why, why? . . . Once I was home at Hayman's Green, I broke down and wept. . . . I stayed

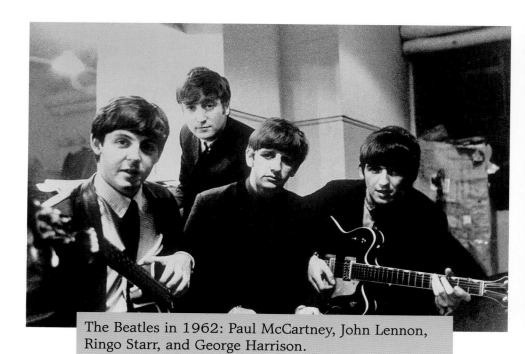

The Beatles in 1962: Paul McCartney, John Lennon, Ringo Starr, and George Harrison.

indoors at [home] for days; numbed, still searching through my mind for a genuine answer to my demise."[3]

Best initially agreed to drum for the band for a few more shows until his predetermined replacement came on board. But then he changed his mind, deciding he did not want to share the stage with the three people he thought he trusted. That is until they had kept the secret of his being fired from him. Best felt betrayed, especially so when he found out he also was friends with his scheduled replacement. It was the drummer for Rory Storm and The Hurricanes, Ringo Starr.

Ringo Starr

He was not born a "Starr," or for that matter a "Ringo." His real name was Richard Starkey, born July 7, 1940, in Liverpool, to Richard and Elsie Starkey. Ritchie, as the boy was known, was raised in a rough area of Liverpool called Dingle, the same section of the city where many of his ancestors had spent their entire lives. His parents had met a few years prior in a bakery where they both worked. When Ritchie was three years old, his parents separated, leaving him and his mother alone at their home. His father remained absent most of his childhood. Minus the second income she had grown accustomed to, Ritchie's mother struggled to pay the bills, and she received government aid to help with necessities. Ritchie said, "Things were pretty tough for Elsie, as I've always called my mother. She tried to bring me up decently. We were poor but never in rags. I was lucky. I was her only child. She could spend more time with me."[4]

Ritchie attended St. Silas' Church of England Primary School. He had not been there long before he said he "felt an awful stab of pain. I remember sweating and being frightened for a while. . . ."[5] Ritchie was taken by ambulance to the hospital with a ruptured appendix, which turned into a more-serious issue. He was placed in intensive care. After two surgeries he recovered, but the considerable amount of time he had spent in the hospital had left him behind in his studies. At eleven, he advanced to Dingle Vale Secondary Modern School, and missed a lot of time there, too, both due to his constant sickness and to his bad habit of skipping school.

At thirteen, Ritchie was hit with a bout of pleurisy, an infection of the membranes surrounding the lungs, sending him back to the hospital until he was fifteen. His hospital stay was brightened by visits from his new stepfather, Harry Graves, a painter and decorator who had married his mother on April 17, 1953. Ritchie emerged from the hospital with little hope of resuming his formal education. He was so far behind in school, that his only option was to get a job. He tried several, but nothing seemed to stick for long until his stepfather secured him a job as an apprentice at an engineering firm.

The American rock and roll craze that had affected so many British youth in the mid-1950s hit Ritchie as well, as did the skiffle craze fueled by the genre's ringleader, Lonnie Donegan. In 1957, Ritchie began his own skiffle group called The Eddie Clayton Skiffle Group. He began by playing rhythm on a basic "skiffle board," and soon his stepfather bought him a secondhand set of drums. When he was eighteen, he moved on to a band called The Raving Texans, which soon morphed into Rory Storm and The Hurricanes. He was with that outfit when he took on the stage name he forever would be known by, Ringo Starr. The first name came about because he liked to wear rings, the last name because he thought "Ringo Starkey" sounded "a bit funny. 'Starr' was a natural. It made sense to me and I liked it. It stuck."[6] His time with Rory Storm and The Hurricanes also helped introduce him to the Beatles when the two Liverpool bands played together in 1960 at the Kaiserkeller club in Hamburg.

> **The first name came about because he liked to wear rings, the last name because he thought 'Ringo Starkey'sounded "a bit funny."**

With his band's permanent—and final—lineup in place, and a recording contract signed, it seemed natural that Lennon would have to focus most of his attention on the Beatles. But domestic matters actually took precedence during this time of his life when he discovered that his girlfriend was pregnant, and he was going to be a father. A few weeks later, August 23, 1962, he and Cynthia Powell went down to the Mount Pleasant Registry Office in Liverpool, and they were married in a short ceremony. No members of Lennon's family attended, not even his aunt Mimi. Lennon said, "I went in the day before [the wedding] to tell Mimi. I said Cyn was having a baby, we were getting married tomorrow, did she want to come? She just let out a groan."[7]

The newlyweds made their home in an apartment owned by Epstein, which he let them use for free as a wedding gift. Despite his rough demeanor, John got high marks as a husband. Cynthia said, ". . . we enjoyed playing husband and wife. He was loving toward me all through my pregnancy, bringing me flowers or little bits and pieces for our home."[8]

Outside his house, Lennon received little credit for playing the husband role well, simply because most people did not know he was married. His marriage was kept under wraps so female fans would think he still was single and continue clamoring to win his affection during his shows.

With Best out and Starr in behind the drum kit, the Beatles returned to Abbey Road Studios in London in September to make their first record for Parlophone. The foursome's takes included a simple number called "Love Me Do," which featured Lennon on harmonica, and another track, "P.S. I Love You." The following month, "Love Me Do" was released to the public as the Beatles' first single.

The "Love Me Do" single, which featured "P.S. I Love You" as its B-side, sold well in the Beatles' hometown of Liverpool, where they already were popular. The song even found its way onto England's record charts, peaking at number seventeen. It was not a stellar showing, but for a new band simply making the charts was a big accomplishment. So was having a song on the radio, and the Beatles were excited to hear themselves on Radio Luxembourg, the Belgian rock and roll broadcast Lennon said had changed his life when he was a teenager. The Beatles also performed on live radio programs and TV shows, and opened two shows for Little Richard, one of the popular American rock and roll singers which originally had helped inspire them to become musicians.

On November 26, the band returned to Abbey Road Studios to record again, this time choosing a song Lennon originally had written as a ballad. It was called "Please Please Me." But Martin was not interested in a slow song as the band's second single, so the four Beatles reworked it, turning it into an all-out rocker clocking in at slightly more than two minutes. When the band finished recording the song, Martin was ecstatic. He said, "Gentlemen, you've just made your first number one record."[9] He was not far off with his early assessment of the song's commercial appeal. "Please Please Me" was released in January 1963, and rose up the charts, buoyed by a performance of the song on the national television show,

John's marriage was kept under wraps so female fans would think he still was single and continue clamoring to win his affection during his shows.

Thank Your Lucky Stars. The song eventually topped out at number two.

Shortly after "Please Please Me" was released, the Beatles set out on their first major tour of Britain, playing venues large and small. At each stop, girls would scream wildly for the band, and opening for them was a difficult task. One singer, whose band had the unenviable task of playing before the Beatles, then introducing them after they were done, said, "I'd only get to mention 'the lads' and a cheer went up. I'd say: 'I'm not bringing *them* on until you're quiet.' There was bedlam. I knew it was a bloodless revolution the music business was experiencing. I'd say 'Ladies and gentlemen, *the lads*,' and the kids would rush the stage. For a virtually unknown group, it was incredible. The game was up."[10]

There was no rest for the weary.

The Beatles entered the recording studio for an eleven-hour session in the middle of February to record enough songs to fill an album. The final product was called *Please Please Me*, after the successful single of the same name, and it was released in Britain on March 22. It was a rush delivery intended to capitalize on the successes of the band's first two singles. The album featured fourteen songs—eight Lennon-McCartney originals and six covers. The album began with the energetic rocker "I Saw Her Standing There" and ended roughly thirty minutes later in complete chaos with a hoarse Lennon screaming the lyrics to a song initially made popular by The Isley Brothers, "Twist and Shout." The song was completed in one take.

There was no rest for the weary. After their recording session, the Beatles returned to the road and continued their rigorous promotional schedule. They even came back to Abbey Road in early March to record their next single. This one, released in April, was called "From Me to You." It was recorded the same month Lennon would return home from tour to discover some life-changing news.

Cynthia Lennon's pregnancy had been a difficult one, filled with loneliness and complicated by health scares. She was so lonely, in fact, that she had agreed to leave the apartment Epstein had provided to move in with John's aunt Mimi, just so she would have some company during the last stages of her pregnancy. John was out of town so much with his band that his wife said, "It was a difficult time. Cold, miserable weather, John was away more than he was at home, Mimi resentful of my presence in the house. And I was about to become a mother—a notion that terrified me."[11]

John Charles Julian Lennon was three days old before his father finally made it to the hospital to see him. Forever to be known as Julian, a derivative of his late grandmother's name, Julia, the Lennons' first child had been born early in the morning on April 8. Cynthia said John "kissed me, then looked at his son, who was in my arms. There were tears in his eyes: 'Cyn, he's bloody marvelous! He's fantastic.' He sat on the bed and I put the baby into his arms. He held each tiny hand, marveling at the miniature fingers, and a big smile spread over his face. 'Who's going to be a famous little rocker like his dad, then?' he said."[12] A few days later, the famous big rocker was back on tour, pretending to be a bachelor, with a newborn baby and a lonely wife at home.

Cynthia now accepted having her husband away from home so frequently. That did not mean she enjoyed it, especially with a new baby to take care of, but she understood his need to tour. It was how he supported his family. She grew up in an environment where men were absent from the home all the time, away at sea for work or off fighting for their country in World War II. Cynthia said, "It was the way things had to be. The message I had received from my parents was that once you were married you stayed together, whatever that entailed. And John and I grew up at a time when it wasn't unusual for women to wait at home for their men. Many Liverpool men went to sea, as John's father had, and their wives had no choice but to wait. My situation was much the same. John was off earning our living and it was my role to be there for him, loving and supportive, when he came home."[13]

She even was supportive when her husband asked her if he could go on vacation to Spain with Epstein, less than three weeks after Julian was born. The Beatles were on a rare break from their rigorous work schedule, and Cynthia said John could go. She said, "I was preoccupied with Julian and nowhere near ready to travel, but I knew how much John needed a break where he wouldn't be recognized and could really relax. I gave them my blessing and they went off together for twelve days."[14] John may not have had the issues of being famous to deal with in Spain, but the trip still managed to create controversy in their lives.

Although he never admitted to it to anyone but his closest friends, it was common knowledge that Epstein was a homosexual, which, at the time, was illegal in England. Lennon knew this, and often had made jokes about it both in and out of Epstein's presence. Neither man seemed to care. McCartney said, "We'd heard that Brian was queer, as we would have called him, nobody used the word 'gay' then. . . . We didn't hold that against him."[15]

But when word got out that he and Epstein had gone on vacation alone together, rumors spread that Lennon also was gay and that he and Epstein were having an affair. Lennon even got into a bloody fight with disc jockey Bob Wooler when Wooler teased him about his relationship with Epstein. Many historians believe some sort of physical intimacy did occur between the two men on their trip, though exactly what has never been determined. Lennon commented on the issue and said, "It was almost a love affair but not quite. It was not consummated but it was a pretty intense relationship."[16]

A few days later, the famous big rocker was back on tour, pretending to be a bachelor, with a new-born baby and a lonely wife at home.

Even controversies such as this could not bring the Beatles down. A fourth single recorded at Abbey Road, "She Loves You," shot straight to number one, eventually selling more than one million copies. The band appeared on radio and television nearly nonstop, and the four members were becoming household names in Britain. Even those who were not rock and roll fans knew who the Beatles were. In large part, that was due to the Beatles' performance before Queen Elizabeth II on November 4 during the Royal Variety Show.

Even in front of the stuffy crowd at the Prince of Wales Theatre in London, the Beatles were their usual playful selves, especially the sarcastic Lennon. After McCartney finished singing "Till There Was You," a song from the play, *The Music Man*, Lennon stepped to the mike and said, "For our last number, I'd like to ask your help. Would the people in the cheaper seats clap your hands? And the rest of you, if you'll just rattle your jewelry. . . ."[17] Lennon, dressed in suit and tie like the rest of his band members, glanced up at the royal box after the last part of his statement, where the queen stood and acknowledged him with a motion of her hand. The band then tore into their version of "Twist and Shout."

As the Beatles' popularity grew, other bands began covering their songs, just as they themselves had done for years. One group that did so was The Rolling Stones, which went on to become a worldwide smash. The Beatles had allowed the Stones—then led by energetic singer Mick Jagger, guitarist Keith Richards, and multi-instrumentalist Brian Woods—to record a song considered to be a throwaway, "I Wanna Be Your Man." It was not a throwaway for the Stones. That band's version reached number twelve on the British charts.

It soon became hard for the Beatles to go out into public without being mobbed. Fans showed up at the band members' homes, often making for some scary situations. Prior to the Beatles' appearance on the extremely popular *Val Parnell's Sunday Night at the London Palladium* TV show, a group of fans lined up outside the studio hoping to get a glimpse of the band. When the band members came out of rehearsal, screaming fans swarmed their car, blocking the path there from the building. The band rushed to the car and dove inside, as fans tried to grab them. After the show, there were two thousand fans outside. The next day, photos of the scene were plastered in every newspaper in London. The *Daily Herald* reported that "screaming girls launched themselves against the police—sending helmets flying and constables reeling."[18] *The Daily Mirror* featured two photos of girls in various states of hysteria, the larger photo showing a girl screaming with her hands on her head, held back by the hands of a security guard. The one-word exclamatory headline at the top of the page succinctly summed up what was happing to Britain: Beatlemania!

"Would the people in the cheaper seat clap your hands? And the rest of you, if you'll just rattle your jewelry . . ."

While rock star Lennon was being accosted by fans, staying in luxury hotels in London and worshipped by thousands, his wife and child were leading a much different life. Cynthia Lennon was back in Liverpool, now living in a rented room with her mother and still keeping her marriage as secret as possible. She said, "Ever since, people have speculated on how I could have put up with it. Was I cowed or afraid of John? Not in the least; I put up with it because I didn't want to do anything to harm John's career, and I had been told repeatedly that going public would do just that. I was loyal to John, and if he needed me to support him by lying low, then that was what I would do."[19]

Her loyalty eventually was rewarded, and in January 1964, she, John, and Julian moved into a three-bedroom apartment in London. She was happy her family finally was living together, but she was not happy with the lack of privacy she had in their new home. Once fans figured out where they lived, they began to pester the Lennons, even camping outside their apartment waiting for someone to come outside. By that time, the Beatles' second album, *With the Beatles*, had been released to overwhelming response. The album, which was a lot less raw than the Beatles' first full-length, featured eight original tracks, including "Don't Bother Me" written by Harrison, "All My Loving," and

> **In mid-January, "I want to Hold Your Hand" entered the top one hundred on the U.S. singles charts.**

the song the band had allowed The Rolling Stones to release, "I Wanna Be Your Man." The album did not include their fifth single, the peppy "I Want to Hold Your Hand," which was released a few days later.

Across the Atlantic Ocean, the Lennons easily could have lived in anonymity anywhere they desired. Popularity in the United States still eluded the band, even after a deal with Vee-Jay Records allowed their records to be released there. "Please Please Me" was the first U.S. release, and it did not do well. In fact, the Beatles were such nobodies that initial pressings of the single misspelled the name of the band as the "Beattles."

Detailed plans were in the works to change all that. Epstein flew to New York in November for several meetings to prepare for the Beatles' first visit to the United States, which he had scheduled for February 1964, when they would perform on the popular *Ed Sullivan Show*. At the time, an appearance on the show meant everything to an act, and easily could make—or break—them. Epstein had arranged for them to play the show twice, which would mean twice the amount of exposure. He also booked a show for them at New York City's prestigious Carnegie Hall. An answer to whether U.S. audiences would embrace the Beatles would certainly come in a few months. But, as it turns out, the band did not have to wait quite that long to find out.

In mid-January, "I Want to Hold Your Hand" entered the top one hundred on the U.S. singles charts. Copies of the record—distributed in America by EMI's subsidiary, Capitol Records—flew off store shelves, eventually selling more than five million copies in the United States alone. During the first week of February, "I Want to Hold Your Hand" hit number one on the charts, and stayed there for seven weeks, until it was knocked off by another Beatles song, "She Loves You."

By that time, the band was already on their way to the States. The promotional machine had beaten them there, plastering word of the Beatles' impending arrival across the country. Both *Time* and *Life* magazines had written about them, and their back catalog of songs was being spun nonstop on radio stations. The frenzy that surrounded the band when they first touched down on American soil on February 7, 1964, was unexpected by some, though it should not have been.

Seventy-three million people watched television on February 9, when the Beatles appeared on *The Ed Sullivan Show* on CBS. It was the most-watched TV program in American history. Significantly fewer people, slightly more than seven hundred, were in the audience to see it live. The Beatles played five songs: "All My Loving," "Till There Was You," "She Loves You," "I Saw Her Standing There," and the chart-topping "I Want to Hold Your Hand." Listeners were treated to an extra, somewhat unexpected, instrument on each song—the chorused screams of the hundreds of young girls in the studio. The band had also taped a second performance earlier that day, which was broadcast on the show two weeks later.

The excitement carried over to the Beatles' first American concert, held two days later at the Coliseum in Washington, D.C., and the following day during two short concerts at Carnegie Hall in New York City. One teen girl who attended one of the Carnegie Hall shows said, "Even when you're screaming, you can still hear. All the reporters in the papers always said you couldn't hear anything with all the noise, but you could, even when you were screaming. Their sexy movements made you scream even louder. They were being sexy with you personally. It was an outlet."[20]

The Beatles returned to England at the end of the month, and in March they began production on their first movie, *A Hard Day's Night*. Band members played themselves in the film, whose plot revolved around what a typical day in the band's life was fancied to be like—trying to avoid screaming fans while staying out of trouble. Beatles' songs played throughout the film, which premiered in London on July 6. It was a box-office smash, and it was also well-reviewed by critics. A music album with the same title as the film was released that summer, as well. Featuring number one singles "A Hard Day's Night" and "Can't Buy Me Love," the record shot straight to the top of the charts and stayed there for

> **Seventy three million people watched television on February 9, when the Beatles appeared on *The Ed Sullivan Show* on CBS.**

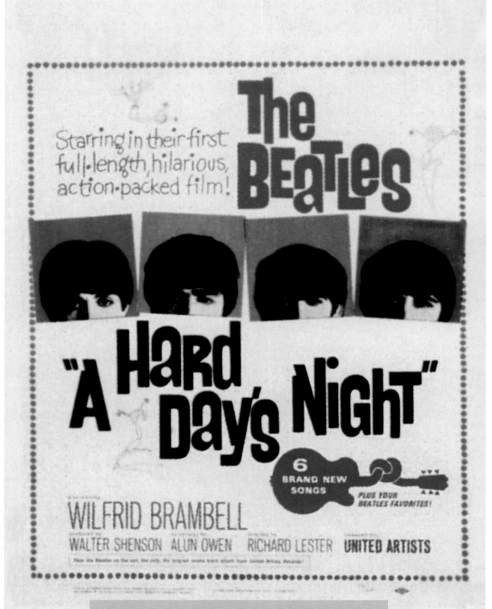

A movie poster for *A Hard Day's Night*.

several weeks. The latter track sold a world-record 2.7 million copies *before* it was even released.

Anything the Beatles were involved in was an instantaneous smash. That included Lennon's first book, which was published in March 1964. Called *In His Own Write*, the book included several of the author's stories, poems, and drawings. Lennon also wrote *A Spaniard in the Works*, which was published a year later. Both were best sellers.

Lennon's fame continued to impact his personal life. Sometimes that was good, sometimes it was bad. One good thing was that he now had enough money to do almost anything he desired, including buying a home south of London in the town of Weybridge. The home was a gigantic Tudor mansion called Kenwood, equipped with more than twenty rooms and a swimming pool. The location offered some privacy for his family, who by then had been constantly besieged by fans at their apartment. Cynthia said, "I couldn't go out, look out of my window or even answer the phone without having to deal with fans, some of whom were clearly crazy. It was just as bad for John. Every time he came home he had to force his way through the girls camped out on our doorstep. . . . [O]bsessive, desperate fans fought, bit and scratched their way to the front to grab any piece of John's clothing they could get hold of."[21] Shortly, Harrison and his girlfriend, Patti Boyd, and Starr and his girlfriend, Maureen, moved into homes near the Lennons'.

Lennon's fame also sparked a reunion with his long-absent father, Alf. For John, this was not a good thing. He had not seen his father since he was five years old—roughly twenty years now—and harbored much hatred toward his pop for having abandoned him as a youngster. As the legend goes, Alf Lennon was working as a dishwasher when one of his coworkers saw a picture of John in a newspaper and pointed it out. That soon led to father and son reuniting on a movie set, where John was filming. According to biographer Bob Spitz, Alf said that he "stuck out my hand to shake his but John just growled at me and said suspiciously, 'What do you want?'"[22] John later said that was because "[h]e turned up after I was famous. . . . He knew where I was all my life—I'd lived in the same house in the same place for most of my childhood, and he knew where."[23]

The next year, Alf Lennon tried to capitalize on the success of his famous son, and he released an album under the name "Freddie Lennon." His first single, "That's My Life," was a flop, and his professional music career ended almost as quickly as it had begun. Father and son did not speak again until just days before Alf Lennon died of stomach cancer in 1976.

Another negative byproduct of Lennon's wealth was that he now had his pick of drugs he previously could not afford. He and the other Beatles had long been recreational users of marijuana, but he now began regularly using LSD. The illegal hallucinogenic drug, also known as acid, impacted nearly every aspect of Lennon's life. Eventually, it would affect his relationship with his

Screaming fans show their admiration of John Lennon and the Beatles in 1964.

family and bandmates, and the type of music he created, but for now it was just another way for him to escape from the rigors of being a star.

In August, the Beatles returned for their first cross-country tour of the United States, beginning in San Francisco on August 19, and ending in New York on September 20. Beatlemania was out in full force on this tour. Because of this, the Beatles kept mostly to their hotel rooms when they were not playing. Even that did not stop creative, and often crazed, fans from attempting to get their hands on the band members. In one instance, on the third stop of the tour August 21 in Seattle, two girls were found hiding under a bed in the Beatles' hotel.[24]

Lennon's newfound introspection began to take its toll on the band.

The Beatles capitalized on their fame by releasing products at a pace that today is nearly unheard of. Their second movie, *Help!* premiered in August 1965, its plot centered around a religious cult trying to retrieve a special ring that has wound up on Starr's finger. The *Help!* album came out the same month, and it included several songs that had appeared in the film. The record's highlights included the title song, as well as "Ticket to Ride" and "You've Got to Hide Your Love Away," a song written by Lennon in a style inspired by American singer-songwriter Bob Dylan. Lennon and the rest of the Beatles had met Dylan on a previous trip to the United States, and Dylan's folkish, personal lyrics had a great impact on Lennon. Until then, the stories he had told through his lyrics were semi-vague and chiefly impersonal, but Dylan's influence helped change that. Through Dylan, Lennon discovered that lyrics can be deep and meaningful. With that revelation, his musical direction changed.

The Dylan influence is evident on *Rubber Soul*, which the Beatles released at the end of 1965. Much of the happy, "she loves you" lyrics the Beatles had become known for were missing from the album, replaced by darker pieces such as "Norwegian Wood" and "Nowhere Man." Lennon's newfound introspection began to take its toll on the band, however, and a rift between Lennon and songwriting partner McCartney began to develop.

Chapter 6

"More Popular..."

Beatlemania suffered a big public relations hit in the summer of 1966, thanks to comments Lennon had made in April to Maureen Cleave, a reporter for the *London Evening Standard* newspaper. When asked about religion, Lennon told Cleave, "Christianity will go. It will vanish and sink. I needn't argue about that. I'm right and will be proved right. We're more popular than Jesus now. I don't know which will go first—rock 'n' roll or Christianity. Jesus was all right, but his disciples were thick and ordinary. It's them twisting it that ruins it for me."[1]

The lengthy article ran in the newspaper, and it was reprinted in others, without ill effects. But when portions of the interview were reprinted out of context in an American teen magazine, it was another story. The magazine, *Datebook*, highlighted the "more popular than Jesus" quote, which set off a chain reaction of anti-Beatles movements across the United States—especially the Southern Bible Belt—and onto other countries, such as South Africa and Spain. Radio stations everywhere stopped playing Beatles records. Groups gathered to burn their records, pictures, and other band-related memorabilia. Numerous death threats were made against Lennon, and the rest of the Beatles, too. The reporter quickly said that the comments were taken out of context, and that Lennon was simply commenting on the state of Christianity as he saw it, with no ill intentions. But it was too late, the damage had been done. Saying he stood behind what he said, Lennon did not want to apologize. Epstein finally talked him into it and Lennon said:

> If I had said television is more popular than Jesus, I might have got away with it, but I just happened to be talking to a friend and I used the words "Beatles" as a remote thing, not as what I think— as Beatles, as those other Beatles like other people see us. I just said "they" are having more influence on kids and things than anything else, including Jesus. But I said it in that way which is the wrong way. . . . I'm not saying that we're better or greater, or comparing us with Jesus Christ as a person or God as a thing or whatever it is. I just said what I said and it was wrong. Or it was taken wrong. And now it's all this. . . . I'm sorry I said it really. I never meant it to be a lousy anti-religious thing. I apologize if that will make you happy. I still don't know quite what I've done. I've tried to tell you what I did do but if you want me to apologize, if that will make you happy, then OK, I'm sorry.[2]

It was not much of an apology, but it was the best Lennon—long known to speak his mind and detest being told not to—could muster.

The controversy began just as the Beatles were about to begin another U.S. tour. The band was as popular as ever, their latest release *Revolver*—with its key songs "Taxman," "Eleanor Rigby," "Got to Get You Into My Life," and "Yellow Submarine"—topping the charts as did everything they released. But the tour was almost canceled because of Lennon's comments. As the band traveled across the country, signs reading "Go Home Beatles" and worse followed them, as did the Beatles burnings and death threats. By the end of the tour, the Beatles were exhausted. After the final show on August 29, 1966, in San Francisco, the band decided they were through touring. The excitement and fun they had in the beginning—playing dives in Hamburg and at the Cavern in Liverpool—had vanished. The band did not want to tour any longer. The Beatles had played their last show.

When they returned to England, the band members went their separate ways. Harrison and his now-wife, Patti, visited India, and they explored the religion of that country. McCartney traveled as well, and he took on various other music projects. Starr and his new wife, Maureen, settled into a quiet life at home.

Lennon was unsure of what to do with his time. He accepted a role in the antiwar film, *How I Won the War*, traveling to Spain to film it. He chopped off his hair and donned wire-rimmed glasses to play the role of Private Gripweed. The short haircut did not stick with him long, but Lennon did like the rounded glasses, and they eventually became his trademark.

When the movie was done filming, Lennon returned to England and became more involved in London's art scene, a move that would change his life as well as the lives of many others. On November 9, he traveled with a friend to the Indica Gallery to see an exhibition titled "Yoko at Indica." Lennon thought the description of the show sounded interesting. His friend had told him "about this Japanese girl from New York, who was going to be in a bag, doing this event or happening."[3] The "Japanese girl" was Yoko Ono, a twice-divorced mother of one, avant-garde artist seven years Lennon's senior. When the two met, Lennon said his friend "introduced me, and of course there was supposed to be this event happening, so I asked, 'Well, what's the event?' She gives me a little card. It just says 'Breathe' on it. And I said, 'You mean [exhaling]?' She says, 'That's it. You've got it.' . . . I got the humour—maybe I didn't get the depth of it but I got a warm feeling from it."[4]

After the final show on August 29, 1966, in San Francisco, the band decided they were through touring.

A short time later, Ono sent Lennon a copy of a book of poetry she had written, *Grapefruit: A Book of Instructions and Drawings*. She also began sending him letters and postcards, and she even visited John and Cynthia's home in Weybridge. Lennon played down his relationship with Ono to his wife. That is, until one day Cynthia came home from a trip to Greece to find the two "sitting on the floor, cross-legged and facing each other, beside a table covered with dirty dishes. They were wearing the terry-cloth robes we kept in the pool house, so I imagined they had been for a swim."[5] Cynthia quickly gathered some belongings and ran out of her home into a taxi that had been waiting outside for her. She returned home a couple days later determined to make her marriage work. But it did not. Cynthia filed for divorce, which was finalized on November 8, 1968. She later married three more times.

During their night spent together, John and Yoko had recorded some strange experimental music, which was released the following year under the title *Unfinished Music No. 1: Two Virgins*. The record was panned by critics and fans alike, and it was most noteworthy for its cover, which featured a black-and-white photograph of Lennon and Ono posing together nude. In 1969, the couple released *Unfinished Music No. 2: Life with the Lions*. By then, Ono had become pregnant with Lennon's child, which she eventually miscarried.

Although they were no longer touring, the Beatles were still a band, albeit without a key member of their team. The "fifth Beatle," as Brian Epstein often was called, was found dead at his home of a drug overdose on August 27, 1967. The Beatles were visiting with Transcendental Meditation guru Maharishi Mahesh Yogi in Bangor, Wales, when they heard of his death. All four Beatles were devastated at the loss of their friend, and they also wondered what the future of the band might be. Lennon later said, "I knew we were in trouble then. I didn't really have any misconceptions about our ability to do anything other than play music, and I was scared. I thought, 'We've . . . had it now.'"[6]

Lennon's assessment proved to be right on. Although holes had been forming in the Beatles' machine for some time, Epstein's death certainly hastened things. Prior to Epstein's death, plans had been in the works to form a corporation called Apple Corps to handle the Beatles' business affairs. The band members took on Apple's leadership role at first, until they discovered they could not handle the business end of things. So they hired their road manager, Neil Aspinall, to do so.

> The "fifth Beatle," as Brian Epstein often was called, was found dead at his home of a drug overdose in August 27, 1967.

Much of the Beatles best work was created the year Epstein died, including *Sgt. Pepper's Lonely Hearts Club Band*, the band's most-experimental album to date. The occasionally psychedelic album was full of hit songs, including "Lucy in the Sky with Diamonds," "With a Little Help from My Friends," and "When I'm Sixty-Four." The album's cover featured wax models of the Beatles and the real Beatles posed among a collage of cardboard models of famous people, including Edgar Allan Poe, Marilyn Monroe, and Albert Einstein. The album was followed by a movie of the same name, though none of the Beatles appeared in the film.

The Beatles in 1967.

At the end of 1967, the Beatles released their *Magical Mystery Tour* album, which continued down the path of experimentation and drug-influenced music. For example, portions of "I Am the Walrus" were written when Lennon was high on LSD, and the lyrics of "Strawberry Fields Forever" talk about how "nothing is real." Other songs on the disc included the more-safe "Hello Goodbye," "All You Need Is Love," and "Penny Lane." The names Strawberry Field and Penny Lane, of course, were places drawn from the Beatles' childhood haunts in Liverpool. A made-for-TV film starring the Beatles called *Magical Mystery Tour* was also made.

Recording sessions for the band's next album, simply titled *Beatles* but better known as *The White Album* because of its all-white cover, did not start off on the right foot. The band had a long-standing policy that wives and girlfriends were not allowed in the studio, but Ono came with Lennon to Abbey Road to record this album. She did not sit idly by, either; instead she offered her critiques of the band members' performances and songs. Needless to say, the three other Beatles had big problems with her being there. They also had all been rather fond of Cynthia, which made matters even worse. The band members' musical tastes had evolved quite a lot during the time they had been together. Lennon's experimental music did not sit well with the others. McCartney's plainness drove Lennon up the wall. Harrison felt his songs were overlooked by the band as a whole, and Starr was so upset that he walked out of the studio for two weeks, threatening to leave the band for good.

Despite all the tumult, *The White Album* was another masterpiece. It shot to the top of the charts in both the United States and Britain, and it became the all-time favorite of many Beatles fans when it was released in November 1968. It was the first full-length album the Beatles had released in nearly a year and a half. The band had released some material in that downtime, most notably "Hey Jude," a song McCartney wrote to Lennon's son, Julian, to help the five-year-old boy through the divorce of his parents. Lennon later said he thought the song was about him. He said, "Ah, it's me. If you think about it, Yoko's just come into the picture. . . . The words 'go out and get her' . . . Subconsciously he was saying 'Go ahead, leave me.' But on a conscious level he didn't want me to go ahead. The angel inside him was saying 'Bless you.' The devil in him didn't like it at all because he didn't want to lose his partner."[7] Either way, the song was a smash. Despite clocking in at a whopping seven minutes and eleven seconds, "Hey Jude" became the number one song in America and stayed on top of the charts for several weeks.

The songs on *The White Album* clearly showed the divide that existed between Lennon and McCartney at the time. As it always was, most of the songwriting credits on *The White Album* were given to the team of Lennon/McCartney, but that was misleading this go-round. Each man basically wrote his own songs, using the other band members as a backing band to

Yoko Ono in 1967.

support them. McCartney highlights included "Back in the U.S.S.R.," "Ob-La-Di, Ob-La-Da," and the raucous "Helter Skelter." Lennon's songs included "Revolution 1," a slowed-down version of the up-tempo "Revolution" that had been released weeks earlier as the B-side to "Hey Jude," and "Julia," an acoustic song he had written about his mother that also included references to Yoko Ono. The double album format even gave the other Beatles room to showcase their tunes. Harrison's classic "While My Guitar Gently Weeps"—featuring Eric Clapton on lead guitar—among them.

By the summer of 1968, Lennon and Ono were completely open with their relationship and often appeared in public together. They moved into an apartment in London's Montagu Square owned by Starr, where they began using drugs frequently, including the often-deadly narcotic, heroin. On October 18, 1968, police raided the apartment looking for drugs. According to one of Lennon's associates, "In one room there was a large trunk full of clothes in which a dog was showing interest. A search of the trunk revealed a small piece of [marijuana]. John and Yoko were asked to go to Marylebone police station where they were formally charged and fingerprinted in my presence."[8] The small amount of money Lennon eventually was fined after he pleaded guilty was negligible, but the damage to his once squeaky-clean reputation was not. Lennon later said he felt as if he was set up: "I guess they didn't like the way the image was looking. The Beatles thing was over. No reason to protect us for being soft and cuddly any more—so bust us! That's what happened."[9]

Although Lennon said it was, the "Beatles thing" was not quite over. There was still more music left in the band. In the spring of 1969, the band released *Yellow Submarine*, a mediocre album that was the soundtrack for a film of the same name. Later that year, they released *Abbey Road*, named after the studio it was made in. That album—which featured "Come Together," and two well-received Harrison songs, "Here Comes the Sun," and "Something"— was released in September. Despite the controversy surrounding Lennon, the album still hit number one in both Britain and in the United States. The album cover, a photo of the band crossing the street to the studio, became one of the most-imitated album covers of all time. Today, there's even a Web cam set up nearby to record what is happening twenty-four hours a day at the popular tourist spot. Once again, Yoko was by Lennon's side in the studio, though she was a bit hobbled at first. Both Lennons had been injured in a car crash July 1, when John lost control of the car he was driving and it ended up in a ditch. John, Yoko, and Yoko's daughter, Kyoko, each had to have stitches to sew up cuts on their faces. Julian, who also had been in the car, was unharmed.

> **By the summer of 1968, Lennon and Ono were completely open with their relationship and often appeared in public together.**

Abbey Road was the last album the Beatles recorded together, but it was not the last Beatles studio album to be released. That distinction goes to *Let It Be*, which the feuding band recorded in January 1969. When the recording was complete, the band was not happy with the final product, and shelved the tapes until a later date. In 1970, those tapes were given to producer Phil Spector, at the suggestion of Lennon, to turn into a finished album. Spector had become well known for his "wall of sound" productions, whereby he would use several instruments playing the same part to create a layered sound. *Let It Be* was released to the public in May 1970, and rode its hit songs "Let It Be," "The Long and Winding Road," and "Get Back" to the top of the charts. Despite its success, McCartney in particular was angry that Spector had been hired to finish the album without his knowledge or consent. He said, "[A] few weeks ago I was sent a re-mixed version of my song 'The Long and Winding Road,' with harps, horns, an orchestra and women's choir added. No one had asked me what I thought. I couldn't believe it."[10] The album was supposed to have hearkened back to the band's roots, with simple music and not a lot of production. The released product was anything but that. In 2003, a new version of the album, called "Let It Be . . . Naked," was released without Spector's embellishments.

Film crews had been present to capture the rehearsing for and recording of *Let It Be*, and caught on tape the tension of the Beatles at the time. Ono again was omnipresent, and she also makes regular

John Lennon and Yoko Ono in 1969 during one of their bed-ins.

appearances in the film. The movie concludes with a short lunchtime concert performed January 30, 1969, on top of the Apple Corps building in London. Keyboardist Billy Preston, who had performed on the album *Let It Be*, sat in on the performance. With their long, shoulder-length hair, mustaches, and beards, the Beatles hardly resembled the squeaky clean lads they were when they burst on the scene some six years earlier. The concert ended when the police shut it down, but not before Lennon had the final words. He said, "I'd like to say thank you on behalf of the group and ourselves, and I hope we passed the audition."[11] It was the last time the Beatles performed together live, and their official breakup was not far behind.

As indicated by her presence in the once-sacred recording studio, Ono was occupying most of Lennon's time at this point. In March, the pair flew to the British territory of Gibraltar, where they wed on March 20. Their honeymoon, as were most events the pair had become involved in, was unconventional. Lennon and Ono traveled to Amsterdam, where they staged a week-long "bed-in for peace" in a hotel room. Reporters were invited to cover the event, which basically consisted of the Lennons lying in bed in their pajamas, talking about

> **Reporters were invited to cover the event, which basically consisted of the Lennons lying in bed in their pajamas, talking about what they thought of war, peace, and more.**

what they thought of war, peace, and more. The following month, Lennon legally changed his middle name, dropping the "Winston" he had following his birth during World War II, and replacing it with "Ono." In May, in Montreal, Canada, the Lennons held a similar bed-in and performed live at a peace concert in Toronto in September.

The Lennons' pro-peace message continued outside their bedroom, as well. In June, Lennon recorded and the next month he released an antiwar song called "Give Peace a Chance," listing "The Plastic Ono Band" as the group's name. The song became a battle cry for the millions of U.S. citizens who were protesting their country's involvement in the Vietnam War. In May, the Beatles released a single written and sung by Lennon called "The Ballad of John and Yoko." The song talked about the couple's marriage and their bed-in, in Amsterdam. In October, Lennon released another single, "Cold Turkey," which talked about heroin addiction and withdrawals.

The peace-loving couple finished the year by installing eleven black-and-white billboards in major cities across the United States that read, "WAR IS OVER! IF YOU WANT IT: Happy Christmas from John & Yoko."

If there was an "official" day that the Beatles breakup occurred, it was September 20, 1969. Band members had gathered in London to sign a favorable new recording contract that had been negotiated for them by their new manager, Allen Klein.

When the four men began discussing what their next move would be, Lennon dropped a bombshell. McCartney recalled Lennon saying, "Well, I wasn't gonna tell you until after we'd signed the Capitol contract. Klein asked me not to tell you. But, seeing as you asked me, I'm leaving the group. . . . It's rather exciting. It's like I remember telling Cynthia I wanted a divorce."[12]

They had no idea that Lennon had quit the band months earlier.

The band members kept Lennon's announcement under wraps for a while, and the general public had no idea what had occurred. When word finally came out, it came from McCartney, which infuriated Lennon who believed McCartney was using the breakup to promote his own album. Included in the press kits for McCartney's first solo album, *McCartney*, released in April 1970, was a series of questions and answers with the artist. Reading McCartney's answers, there was no doubt the Beatles were through. The media went wild with the story, attributing the break up to McCartney leaving the Beatles. They had no idea that Lennon had quit the band months earlier.

Over the years, the breakup of the Beatles has been blamed on many things: poor business deals; McCartney's wife, Linda; George Harrison's quest for more musical input; drugs. But the most-frequently blamed reason was Yoko Ono, and many people hated her for it.

Chapter 7

Death of a Legend

The finality of the Beatles' breakup affected each band member differently. George Harrison was already well on the way to a successful solo career, occasionally assisted in that quest by Starr, who also began releasing his own material. McCartney's first solo record sold well, and he began working on another one with his wife.

Lennon eventually released more music of his own, but he also spent his time pursuing other ventures. He had become fascinated by *The Primal Scream*, a book by California psychotherapist Arthur Janov, and he decided to fly to Los Angeles to work with Janov. He and Yoko spent a few months in California, participating in Janov's "Primal Scream" therapy class—where the patient would lie on the floor, think about bad events that had occurred in his or her life, and scream about them. The idea was to release all the pent-up pain and anger inside.

When he returned to England, Lennon began to refocus on his music, and in December 1970, released his first solo album, *John Lennon/Plastic Ono Band*. The highly personal album includes songs about the loss of his mom—"Mother," and "My Mummy's Dead"—and others about abandonment, love, and religion. The album was praised by critics, but did nothing to stop his zany behavior.

On April 23, 1971, he and Yoko tried to kidnap her daughter, Kyoko, from her father and Yoko's ex-husband, Tony Cox, who had custody of Kyoko. Detectives had tracked Cox to Spain, and the Lennons flew there and took Kyoko when she was at school. The police arrested the kidnappers and detained them for several hours. In the end, Kyoko was asked who she would rather be with. It was exactly what had happened to Lennon when he was a child. Kyoko chose her father and stepmother, and John and Yoko were released and flew back home.

The nastiness of the Beatles' breakup came to a head in 1971, when McCartney sued to end the Beatles' partnership. A judge ruled in McCartney's favor a few years later. But the individual recordings kept coming. At the end of 1971, Lennon released his second solo effort, *Imagine*, which he had recorded at Tittenhurst, the expansive Georgian mansion outside London he and Yoko had moved into in 1969. As Lennon's previous release had been, *Imagine* was full of introspective, thought-provoking, tender songs. Included among them was the title song, which continued Lennon's pro-peace message. Recording the album was one of the last noteworthy moves Lennon made at Tittenhurst, and even in England for that matter. By the time *Imagine* was released in early September, he and Yoko were in New York City.

John and Yoko decided to come to New York for various reasons. Escaping the stress the couple faced in England was one, following Kyoko to the United States to continue trying to gain custody of the girl was another. They soon moved to Greenwich Village in New York City, where they would hang out in their apartment with many of the leaders of the Youth International Party (YIPPIE), a radical political group founded by activists such as Abbie Hoffman and Jerry Rubin. Drugs of all types were commonplace, including cocaine, heroin, and marijuana.

Lennon's involvement with the left-wing group placed him under the watchful eye of the government, which wanted to deport him back to England because they felt he was a threat to national security. The FBI even got involved, following Lennon around, tapping his phone, and filing reports on his activities. The government received thousands of letters of support for Lennon, and the government eventually backed off its calls for deportation.

The FBI even got involved, following Lennon around, tapping his phone, and filing reports on his activities.

Lennon had enough problems to deal with even without the government's harassment. His third solo album, 1972's angry *Some Time in New York City*, was a flop by Beatles standards. Lennon's relationship with Yoko also was suffering. In an attempt to respark it, the couple moved from Greenwich Village to a luxurious apartment building near Central Park called the Dakota. The move did not help their relationship much. The passion had all but left it. The couple decided they needed a break from each other, and Yoko suggested John head to Los Angeles for a while. When he said he did not want to travel alone, she suggested he take their assistant, a twenty-two-year-old Chinese-American woman named May Pang, with him. The trip did not turn out to be a short one.

Lennon and Pang spent the next fourteen months in Los Angeles, a period of time that Lennon would eventually call his "lost weekend." His fourth solo album, *Mind Games*, was released shortly after he arrived on the West Coast, and sold relatively well, especially compared to his previous effort. His fifth solo album, 1974's *Walls and Bridges*, produced a number one single, the collaboration with pop musician Elton John called "Whatever Gets You Through the Night." The song even brought Lennon out of his unofficial retirement to perform on stage again, which he did with Elton John on Thanksgiving Day 1974, at Madison Square Garden in New York City. The pair also played two Beatles songs, "Lucy in the Sky with Diamonds" and "I Saw Her Standing There."

Lennon and Pang returned to New York in February 1975, but they were not immediately welcomed back at

John Lennon in New York City in 1974.

the Dakota. Yoko still was not ready to live with her husband again, but eventually she caved in. She said, "We were in our bedroom and John said, 'So I really burnt the bridge, right? You won't let me come back.' And it was said in such a way that I said, 'Okay, you can come back.' I was thinking to myself, 'What am I saying?' but I couldn't help it."[1]

Yoko became pregnant shortly after their reconciliation, and on October 9, 1975, she gave birth to Sean Taro Ono Lennon. The boy's first name was the Irish version of the name "John," and his middle name was the Japanese name commonly given to one's firstborn child. He was born on his father's thirty-fifth birthday to a forty-two-year-old mother who had stayed in bed during most of her pregnancy because of her advanced age and history of miscarriages.

Sean's birth domesticated Lennon, who shunned his old drinking and drugging buddies altogether, replacing them with days with his family inside their apartment. Even music took a backseat to the raising of Sean. After the release of *Rock 'n' Roll*, an album of Lennon singing 1950s- and 1960s-era songs, such as "Stand By Me," "Ain't That a Shame," and "Peggy Sue," Lennon mostly disappeared from the music scene, and did not release another album for five years. He even somewhat reconciled with McCartney, who would call and, eventually, stop by the Lennons' when he was in town. McCartney said, "It was better to talk about cats, or baking bread, or babies [rather than business]. So we did that, and I had a lot in common with him because we were having our babies and I was into a similar sort of mode. So the air cleared and I was able to speak to him and go and see him."[2]

In 1976, Lennon received his green card, allowing him to become a permanent resident of the United States. His first extended trip outside his apartment came a year later, when he, Sean, and Yoko traveled to Japan to spend time with Yoko's family. They spent four months there, basking in the freedom of not being recognized. When they returned to New York, Lennon continued doing many of the duties traditionally thought of as motherly. Sean, and age, had changed Lennon's life in many ways. The hard-core drug use he had done prior to Sean's birth was no more. In a sense he was a recluse. To many, this made him even more fascinating than he ever had been. Now, there was a mystery about him. Would he ever perform in public again? Would he ever release another album? Would the Beatles ever reunite?

One of the questions was answered in the fall of 1980, when Lennon released what was scheduled to be his big comeback record. He began writing the record over the summer during a trip to Bermuda with his family. When he returned home, he began recording the songs at a New York studio called the Hit Factory. Ono also had written several songs of her own, and she recorded

> In a sense he was a recluse. To many, this made him even more fascinating than he ever had been. Now, there was a mystery about him.

Lennon and his son, Sean, in the late 1970s.

them, too. The end result was *Double Fantasy*, released November 17, 1980. The disc featured eight Yoko songs and eight of John's, mostly introspective pop songs about his life and family. "(Just Like) Starting Over," and "Woman" were for Yoko; "Beautiful Boy (Darling Boy)" was for Sean; and "Watching the Wheels" was for his fans, a musical answer to the countless questions he received as to why he had taken so much time away from the spotlight. The album was a success. Lennon's fans were happy he was back, and the Lennons even began giving interviews to certain members of the media. Lennon was inspired, and, on many days, made regular trips to the studio to do more work. December 8, 1980, was one such day.

As usual, Lennon left the Dakota late in the day. Shortly after 5 P.M., as he headed out the front doors of the building, he stopped to sign a copy of *Double Fantasy* for a fan. Lennon wrote: "John Lennon 1980," and he climbed into his limousine and rode to the studio. Some five hours later, Lennon returned home, climbed out of the limo, and headed back into the building. That is when he heard a man call his name. As Lennon was turning to see who it was, the man shot him five times in the back. Lennon wobbled into the Dakota's security office and moaned, "I'm shot, I'm shot."[3] When the police arrived, Lennon was loaded into the back of a squad car and taken to the hospital. It was too late. He had lost too much blood, and he was pronounced dead on arrival. He was forty years old.

Back at the Dakota, Lennon's killer had calmly sat on the sidewalk after the shooting, holding a copy of J. D. Salinger's classic novel, *The Catcher in the Rye*. He did not resist as the police escorted him into the squad car. It was the same fan that, hours earlier, Lennon had signed a copy of his album for. His name was Mark David Chapman, a twenty-five-year-old former security guard who had traveled from Hawaii just to kill Lennon. Chapman later pleaded guilty to second-degree murder and was sentenced to twenty years to life in prison. He has come up for parole several times, and he has been denied each time.

Reaction to Lennon's death was immediate. Television stations interrupted their late-night broadcasts to announce what little information they had, much of which later turned out to be erroneous. Distraught and in shock, Yoko soon issued a brief statement to the media saying that there would be no funeral. The grieving widow asked that people across the world simply spend ten minutes honoring Lennon at exactly 2 P.M. on December 14.

McCartney first learned of Lennon's death from a phone call, and he was too distraught to speak. Reporters soon gathered at his home looking for comments, but even the next day, McCartney was too upset to speak much about it. He said, "I can't take it in at the moment. John was a great man, who'll be remembered for his unique contributions to art, music and world peace."[4] McCartney spent several days in the studio, focusing his mind on work to help keep it off

Crowds gather outside of the Dakota on December 9,
1980, after John Lennon was shot.

the terrible tragedy. He also worried for a long time that he might be the next Beatle to be killed.

There may not have been a funeral, but fans still needed a place to gather and mourn the loss of the most-famous Beatle. They did so in cities across the world. In New York, thousands of people gathered outside the Dakota, singing "Give Peace a Chance," and other Lennon songs. Many camped out across the street in Central Park until the December 14 vigil, when more than one hundred thousand people showed up. The United States had not seen a mass mourning like this since 1963, when President Kennedy was assassinated. Ironically, it had been the music of Lennon and the rest of the Beatles that helped the country's grieving process during that time. Today, people still gather at Central Park on the anniversary of his death and his birthday, only now the place where they gather has a more-meaningful name than it did the first time they gathered there. In 1981, the City of New York voted to rename a two-and-one-half-acre portion of Central Park as Strawberry Fields, after the Beatles song. A few years later, Yoko donated one million dollars to landscape and maintain the park. Today, Strawberry Fields features a large mosaic piece of art with the word "Imagine" in the middle of it.

Chapter 8

The Music Lives on

Music helped many people heal after Lennon's death, including his three former bandmates. George Harrison wrote a song about Lennon, "All Those Years Ago," the year after Lennon's death, with Paul McCartney singing backing vocals. McCartney released his own tribute song, "Here Today," in 1982. Julian Lennon, who was seventeen at the time of his father's death, went on to become a musician, too, and wrote "Too Late for Goodbyes" for his dad, and the song was included on his first album, *Valotte*, which was released in 1984. Julian's half brother, Sean, also took to a career in music, both as a solo musician and as a member of others' bands, including Cibo Matto and, more recently, The Ghost of a Saber Toothed Tiger.

The year after Lennon's death, Yoko Ono began a romantic relationship with an antique dealer turned artist named Sam Havadtoy, and she remained with him until 2001. She continued to release music and art

Fans gather during an anniversary of Lennon's death in Strawberry Fields in Central Park in New York City.

A closeup of the "Imagine" mosaic.

projects, and she also worked to carry on the legacy of her late husband, no small task considering the legend he has become. That legacy includes handling Lennon's share of the Beatles' affairs, which often led to her feuding with the other band members, especially McCartney, whom Lennon shared songwriting credits with. More recently, Yoko and McCartney have appeared together in public several times.

McCartney continued on with his music, as well, and went on to become the most-successful songwriter in history, having written or co-written 188 records that made it on the charts. Of those, 91 hit the top ten and 33 went to number one.[1] McCartney's wife, Linda, died in 1998 of breast cancer, the same disease that had taken his mother's life when he was a boy. In 2002, he married model Heather Mills and they divorced in 2008.

Harrison released a total of eleven solo albums after the Beatles broke up, and he had a few number one singles. In the late 1980s, he formed a rock and roll supergroup called the Traveling Wilburys, with Bob Dylan, Jeff Lynne, Roy Orbison, and Tom Petty. He was not the first Beatle to have formed a supergroup. That honor actually went to Lennon, who in 1968 had performed with Eric Clapton of Cream, Mitch Mitchell of The Jimi Hendrix Experience, and Keith Richards of The Rolling Stones in a one-off performance for a TV special in a band called The Dirty Mac. In 2002, another all-star band—including McCartney and Starr—

In 2009, *Beatles: Rock Band* hit the stores.

formed to honor Harrison, who had died of brain cancer on November 29, 2001, at the age of fifty-eight.

Like the other Beatles, Starr continued releasing music after Lennon's death, even touring with several different lineups under the name Ringo Starr & His All-Starr Band. In the mid-1980s, he acted as both narrator and conductor of the popular TV show, *Thomas the Tank Engine and Friends*, and he also has been involved in numerous film projects—as an actor, producer, director, and more. Starr's son, Zak Starkey, became a drummer, too, and performed with The Who, Oasis, and others.

In the years immediately following Lennon's death, fans continued to clamor for a reunion of the remaining Beatles. It never happened. However, the three remaining Beatles did reunite in the studio one time, in 1994. That happened after Yoko gave the band members some tapes of songs Lennon had recorded years earlier. The Beatles took the tapes, recorded their own parts to them, and completed two songs: "Free as a Bird," and "Real Love." The songs were released in the mid-1990s on separate *Anthology* compilation albums. That same year, Lennon was inducted into the Rock and Roll Hall of Fame as a solo artist. The Beatles had received the same honor six years earlier.

The Beatles now have sold 170 million records in the United States alone. That is fifty million more than Elvis Presley, the man whose music helped inspire each of the Beatles to begin playing music in the first place, and the person Lennon said he always aspired to be bigger than. He succeeded in that quest. Worldwide, the Beatles have

Julian Lennon and Sean Lennon

sold more than one billion records. Both those sales numbers are world records, and they are not the only ones the band holds. In 2000, the Beatles set another one when 13.5 million copies of their album *1*, which features nearly every song the band released that had topped either the U.S. or British sales charts. And that was more than thirty years after the band had officially broken up. The Beatles marketing continues to this day. In September 2009, *Beatles: Rock Band* was released to the public, and the band's entire music catalog was remastered, too. The band also has won nine Grammy Awards.

In death, Lennon has become an icon. Kids whose parents were not even born when Lennon was alive recognize his name and picture, and even more know his songs. His songs have become inspirational anthems repeatedly played during difficult times. Times of despair. Times of struggle. Times of war. How different might music, and perhaps the world, be if a crazed fan had not prematurely ended Lennon's life? All one can do is imagine.

Chronology

1940—John Winston Lennon born October 9 in Liverpool, England, to Alfred "Alf" and Julia Lennon; Ringo Starr born

1942—James Paul McCartney born

1943—George Harold Harrison born

1945—His parents separated, John goes to live with his aunt and uncle, George and Mimi Smith, at Mendips

1952—Enters Quarry Bank High School

1955—John's uncle, George Smith, dies

1956—John's mother buys him his first guitar; forms first band, eventually to be known as The Quarrymen

1957—Meets Paul McCartney, asks him to join group; begins attending Liverpool College of Art

1958—Meets George Harrison, asks him to join group; records music for first time; mother, Julia, struck and killed by automobile

1960—Stuart Sutcliffe and Pete Best join The Quarrymen; band changes its name to the Beatles; Beatles begin residency in Hamburg, Germany

1961—Stuart Sutcliffe quits the band, necessitating Paul McCartney's switch from guitar to bass; Beatles meet future manager Brian Epstein

1962—Stuart Sutcliffe dies; Ringo Starr replaces Pete Best on drums; Lennon weds longtime girlfriend Cynthia Powell

1963—First Beatles album, *Please Please Me*, released; son John Charles Julian Lennon born April 8

1964—Beatles perform on *The Ed Sullivan Show* and begin first tour of United States; publishes first book, *In His Own Write*

1965—Publishes second book, A *Spaniard in the Works*

1966—Criticized for saying the Beatles are "more popular than Jesus"; plays role in film, *How I Won the War*; meets artist Yoko Ono

1967—Beatles manager Brian Epstein dies of drug overdose

1968—Divorce from Cynthia is finalized; arrested, along with Yoko Ono, for drug possession; releases experimental album with Ono called *Two Virgins*

1969—Marries Yoko Ono; stages two "bed-ins for peace" with Yoko Ono; Beatles officially break up; Lennon records "Give Peace a Chance" with Ono

1970—Releases first solo album, *John Lennon/Plastic Ono Band*

1971—Releases second solo album, *Imagine*; moves to New York City

1972—Releases third solo album, *Some Time in New York City*; FBI begins monitoring Lennon's activities

1973—Separates from Yoko Ono and moves to Los Angeles with assistant May Pang

1975—Moves back to New York apartment with Yoko Ono; son Sean Taro Ono Lennon born October 9

1976—Lennon receives his green card, allowing him to become a permanent resident of the United States

1980—Releases *Double Fantasy* album; shot and killed outside his apartment by Mark David Chapman on December 8

1988—Beatles inducted into Rock and Roll Hall of Fame

1994—Inducted into Rock and Roll Hall of Fame as a solo artist

Discography

Selected Solo Discography

Unfinished Music No. 1: *Two Virgins* (1968)

Unfinished Music No. 2: *Life with the Lions* (1969)

Wedding Album (1969)

John Lennon/Plastic Ono Band (1970)

Imagine (1971)

Some Time in New York City (1972)

Mind Games (1973)

Walls and Bridges (1974)

Shaved Fish (1975)

Rock 'n' Roll (1975)

Double Fantasy (1980)

The John Lennon Collection (1982)

Milk and Honey (1984)

Live In New York City (1986)

Menlove Avenue (1986)

Lennon Legend: The Very Best of John Lennon (1998)

Anthology (1998)

Glossary

avant-garde—Experimental

constable—A British police officer

corporal punishment—Physical punishment exacted on someone accused of a crime

extramarital—Something occurring outside the marriage, such as an affair

green card—A document given to an individual allowing them to become a permanent resident of the United States

hemorrhage—A discharge of a large amount of blood from the blood vessels

introspection—The act of examining ones own feelings and thoughts

mastectomy—Surgical removal of all or part of a breast, often performed as a treatment for cancer

monolith—A large single block of stone

shrapnel—Bomb fragments

skiffle—A style of music featuring rudimentary instruments such as washboards and jugs popular in Britain during the 1950s

stucco—A type of plaster or cement finish used on the inside or outside wall of a home

subsidiary—A company that is subordinate to another

Teddy boy—The name given to rebellious British youth of the 1950s who often wore long jackets, skinny ties and short-legged pants

tête-à-tête—A private conversation between two people

Chapter Notes

Chapter 1: Coming to America

1. Cynthia Lennon, *John* (New York: Crown, 2005), p. 131.
2. Hunter Davies, *The Beatles* (New York: McGraw-Hill, 1978), p. 195.
3. Ibid.
4. Peter Shotton and Nicholas Schaffner, *John Lennon in My Life* (New York: Stein and Day, 1983), p. 89.
5. Phillip Norman, *John Lennon: The Life* (New York: HarperCollins, 2008), p. 342.
6. Lennon, p. 132.
7. Norman, p. 343.
8. Bob Spitz, *The Beatles: The Biography* (New York: Little, Brown and Company, 2005), p. 459.
9. Ibid., p. 460.
10. "The Beatles: The First U.S. Visit," August 14, 2007, <http://www.youtube.com/watch?v=jYciRQDkYD4> (July 6, 2009).
11. Jann S. Wenner, *Lennon Remembers* (London: Verso, 2000), p. 20.

Chapter 2: Genius and Pain

1. Bob Spitz, *The Beatles: The Biography* (New York: Little, Brown and Company, 2005), p. 24.
2. Rod Davis, "Was John Lennon born during an air raid?" September 2006, <http://liverpoolbeatlescene.com/air.html> (August 5, 2009).

3. Prem Willis-Pitts, Liverpool, *The Fifth Beatle* (Littleton, Colo.: Amozen Press, 2000), p. 10.
4. Phillip Norman, *John Lennon: The Life* (New York: HarperCollins, 2008), pp. 9–10.
5. Spitz, p. 21.
6. Ibid., p. 20.
7. Julia Baird with Geoffrey Giuliano, *John Lennon, My Brother* (New York: Henry Holt and Co., 1988), p. 9.
8. Spitz, p. 28.
9. Ibid.
10. Norman, p. 21.
11. Hunter Davies, *The Beatles* (London: Cassell Illustrated, 1996), p. 12.
12. Ibid.
13. Ibid., p. 9.
14. Baird with Giuliano, p. 13.
15. Spitz, p. 33.
16. Phillip Norman, *Shout: The Beatles in Their Generation* (New York: Fireside, 2003), p. 9.
17. Peter Shotton and Nicholas Schaffner, *John Lennon in My Life* (New York: Stein and Day, 1983), p. 20.
18. Davies, p. 13.
19. Shotton and Schaffner, p. 31.
20. Ibid., p. 32.
21. Norman, p. 12.
22. Jann S. Wenner, *Lennon Remembers* (London: Verso, 2000), p. 36.
23. Baird with Giuliano, p. 23.
24. Shotton and Schaffner, p. 37.
25. Baird with Giuliano, p. 19.

26. Spitz, p. 35.

27. Shotton and Schaffner, p. 49.

28. Norman, p. 88.

29. Shotton and Schaffner, p. 67.

30. Beatles, *The Beatles Anthology* (San Francisco: Chronicle, 2000), p. 12.

Chapter 3: Becoming the Beatles

1. Geoffrey Giuliano, *Blackbird: The Life and Times of Paul McCartney* (New York: DaCapo Press, 1997), p. 11.

2. Barry Miles, *Paul McCartney: Many Years From Now* (New York: Henry Holt and Co., 1997), p. 10.

3. Ibid., p. 19.

4. Ibid., p. 20.

5. Ibid., p. 21.

6. Phillip Norman, *John Lennon: The Life* (New York: HarperCollins, 2008), p. 109.

7. Ibid.

8. Bob Spitz, *The Beatles: The Biography* (New York: Little, Brown and Company, 2005), p. 109.

9. Peter Shotton and Nicholas Schaffner, *John Lennon in My Life* (New York: Stein and Day, 1983), p. 58.

10. Ibid.

11. Joshua M. Greene, *The Spiritual and Musical Journey of George Harrison* (Hoboken, N.J.: Wiley & Sons, 2006), p. 2.

12. Ibid., p. 3.

13. Ibid., p. 11.

14. Miles, pp. 31–32.

15. Julia Baird with Geoffrey Giuliano, *John Lennon, My Brother* (New York: Henry Holt and Co., 1988), p. 44.
16. Ibid.
17. Ibid., pp. 44–45.
18. Miles, p. 49.
19. Ibid.
20. Norman, pp. 154–155.
21. Cynthia Lennon, *John* (New York: Crown, 2005), p. 18.
21. Ibid., p. 19.
23. Spitz, pp. 132–133.
24. Ibid., p. 135.
25. Colin Hanton, "John Lennon's Original Quarrymen," <http://www.originalquarrymen.co.uk/html/colin.html> (August 12, 2009).
26. Pete Best and Patrick Doncaster, *Beatle! The Pete Best Story* (London: Plexus, 2001), p. 13.
27. Ibid., p. 16.
28. Ibid., p. 29.

Chapter 4: Made in Germany

1. Hunter Davies, *The Beatles* (London: Cassell Illustrated, 1996), p. 43.
2. Ibid., p. 76.
3. Ibid., pp. 76–77.
4. Ibid., p. 77.
5. Cynthia Lennon, *John* (New York: Crown, 2005), p. 55.
6. Ibid.
7. Ray Coleman, *Lennon: The Definitive Biography* (London: Pan Books, 1992), p. 210.

8. Ibid., p. 213.
9. Ibid., pp. 214–215.
10. Barry Miles, *Paul McCartney: Many Years From Now* (New York: Henry Holt and Co., 1997), p. 67.
11. Davies, p. 89.
12. Ibid.
13. Davies, pp. 92–93.
14. Coleman, p. 251.
15. Pete Best and Patrick Doncaster, *Beatle! The Pete Best Story* (London: Plexus, 2001), p. 83.
16. Miles, p. 74.
17. John Lennon, "Being a Short Diversion on the Dubious Origins of Beatles," *Mersey Beat*, July 6, 1961, <http://www.beatletour.com/d_mersey_beat.htm> (August 2, 2009).
18. Bob Spitz, *The Beatles: The Biography* (New York: Little, Brown and Company, 2005), p. 266.
19. Miles, p. 85.
20. Coleman, p. 251.
21. Phillip Norman, *John Lennon: The Life* (New York: HarperCollins, 2008), p. 263.
22. Coleman, pp. 251–252.
23. Norman, p. 263.
24. Coleman, p. 258.

Chapter 5: Beatlemania Spreads

1. Malcolm Doney, *Lennon and McCartney* (New York: Hippocrene Books, 1981), p. 30.
2. Pete Best and Patrick Doncaster, *Beatle! The Pete Best Story* (London: Plexus, 2001), p. 165.
3. Ibid., pp 166–167.

4. Alan Clayson, *Ringo Starr: Straight Man or Joker?* (New York: Paragon House, 1996), pp. 18–19.

5. Ibid., p. 22.

6. Ibid., p. 56.

7. Hunter Davies, *The Beatles* (London: Cassell Illustrated, 2004), p. 201.

8. Cynthia Lennon, *John* (New York: Crown, 2005), p. 98.

9. Bob Spitz, *The Beatles: The Biography* (New York: Little, Brown and Company, 2005), p. 360.

10. Ray Coleman, *Lennon: The Definitive Biography* (London: Pan Books, 1995), pp. 301–302.

21. Lennon, p. 107.

21. Ibid., p. 113.

22. Ibid., pp. 106–107.

23. Ibid. p. 115.

24. Barry Miles, *Paul McCartney: Many Years From Now* (New York: Henry Holt and Co., 1997), p. 88.

25. Spitz, p. 404.

26. "The Beatles—The Royal Variety Performance," November 24, 2007, <http://www.youtube.com/watch?v=AXlvhEjDbxE> (August 12, 2009).

27. Spitz, p. 428.

28. Lennon, pp. 122–123.

29. Davies, p. 243.

30. Lennon, p. 149.

31. Spitz, p. 497.

32. Ibid.

33. Casey McNerthney, "Beatles stay at Edgewater helped mark its place in history," *The Seattle Post-Intelligencer*, August 20, 2009, <http://www.seattlepi.com/local/409468_beatles21.html> (August 21, 2009).

Chapter 6: "More Popular . . ."

1. Bob Spitz, *The Beatles: The Biography* (New York: Little, Brown and Company, 2005), p. 615.

2. "John Lennon's bigger than Jesus statement— in context," <http://beatlesnumber9.com/biggerjesus.html> (August 12, 2009).

3. Phillip Norman, *John Lennon: The Life* (New York: HarperCollins, 2008), p. 466.

4. Ibid., p. 478

5. Cynthia Lennon, *John* (New York: Crown, 2005), p. 213

6. Norman, pp. 507–508.

7. Ibid., p. 565.

8. Ray Coleman, *Lennon: The Definitive Biography* (London: Pan Books, 1995), p. 481.

9. Ibid., p. 482.

10. Barry Miles, *Paul McCartney: Many Years From Now* (New York: Henry Holt and Co., 1997), p. 575.

11. Beatles: "*Let It Be*, Part 9," August 24, 2007, <http://www.youtube.com/watch?v=CigrtARXXb4&feature=PlayList&p=D50AA48887FCA192&index=86> (August 10, 2009).

12. Miles, p. 561.

Chapter 7: Death of a Legend

1. Phillip Norman, *John Lennon: The Life* (New York: HarperCollins, 2008), p. 743.

2. Barry Miles, *Paul McCartney: Many Years From Now* (New York: Henry Holt and Co., 1997), pp. 590–591.
3. Ray Coleman, *Lennon: The Definitive Biography* (London: Pan Books, 1995), p. 701.
4. Miles, p. 593.

Chapter 8: The Music Lives On

1. "Guinness World Records Launches 2009 Edition," September 17, 2008, <http://www.guinnessworld-records.com/news/2008/09/080916.aspx> (August 12, 2009).

Further Reading

Anderson, Jennifer Joline. *John Lennon: Legendary Musician & Beatle*. Edina, MN.: Abdo Publishing Company, 2010.

Duggleby, John. *Revolution: The Story of John Lennon*. Greensboro, N.C.: Morgan Reynolds, 2007.

Edgers, Geoff. *Who Were The Beatles?* New York: Grosset & Dunlap, 2006.

Lalani, Zane.*Teenagers Guide To The Beatles*. Tampa, FL: AverStream Press, 2005.

Partridge, Elizabeth. *John Lennon: All I Want Is The Truth: A Biography*. New York, NY: Viking, 2005.

Stevens, John. *The Songs of John Lennon: The Beatle Years*. Boston, Mass.: Berklee Press Publications, 2002.

Internet Addresses

John Lennon

<http://www.rockhall.com/inductee/
  john-lennon>

John Lennon: The Official Site

<http://www.johnlennon.com>

Index

10/14
28.49

replacement   C.1

DATE DUE

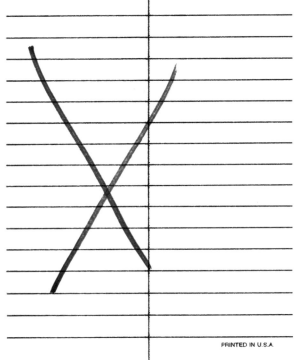

PRINTED IN U.S.A.